Studio Dreamshare created these projects on the traditional and unceded territory of the Algonquin Anishinaabeg. Today, this land is home to many Indigenous people from across Turtle Island, and we acknowledge the shared opportunity to live and work within this beautiful territory.

We acknowledge that Indigenous peoples—particularly the Algonquin—have been stewards of this land since time immemorial. As such, we treat the land, its plants, animals, stories and people with honour and respect, as reflected in the environmental theme of our works.

Recognition of the vast contributions and historic importance of Indigenous peoples must also be clearly and overtly connected to our collective commitment to making the promise and challenge of Truth and Reconciliation real in our communities.

Dorian Pearce *Community Activist*

Greetings

Reverend Tiina Cote, EcoPembroke

Welcome to this publication of unique creative environmental activism by the young and young at heart. The seeds for this activism were planted in the 2021 *Glimpses of Tomorrow* Intergenerational Photovoice Art Camp, a joint venture between Studio Dreamshare and EcoPembroke. The ground that would nourish those seeds was enriched by the growing local understanding that art is a powerful tool which prompts questions and initiates conversations about environmental concerns, thus empowering participants and observers to create positive change.

Since last summer, many intergenerational hands and organizations emerged to nurture those seeds of activism, including Artist Facilitator Catherine Moeller of Clay Paper Theatre in Toronto and Registered Social Worker Julianna Morin of Good Call Counselling Services in Pembroke. We are blessed with the creative passions of these and many other individuals who brought their skills and time, their spiritual and cultural elements to create such a web of Earth care.

The metaphorical tending of these seeds produced the unique community engagements represented in this publication: *Jubilee Tea*, an interactive character development workshop resulting in a short film; *The River is Sacred*, an Intergenerational Community Art Camp in which participants created a puppet street performance that kicked off CultureFest in downtown Pembroke, incorporating recycled materials to tell the story of a river that is healed by a group of caring river animals; and the literal planting of seeds and nourishing of plants with the EcoPembroke seeds and planting community garden project.

Caring for our earth and for each other remains fundamental to the evolving environmental activism in Pembroke and the Upper Ottawa Valley.

Thank you again for the generous funding support from the Eastern Ontario Outaouais Regional Council of The United Church of Canada, and the many individuals who donated or purchased that which was needed for the 2022 Community Engagements. EcoPembroke can be reached at ecopembroke@gmail.com.

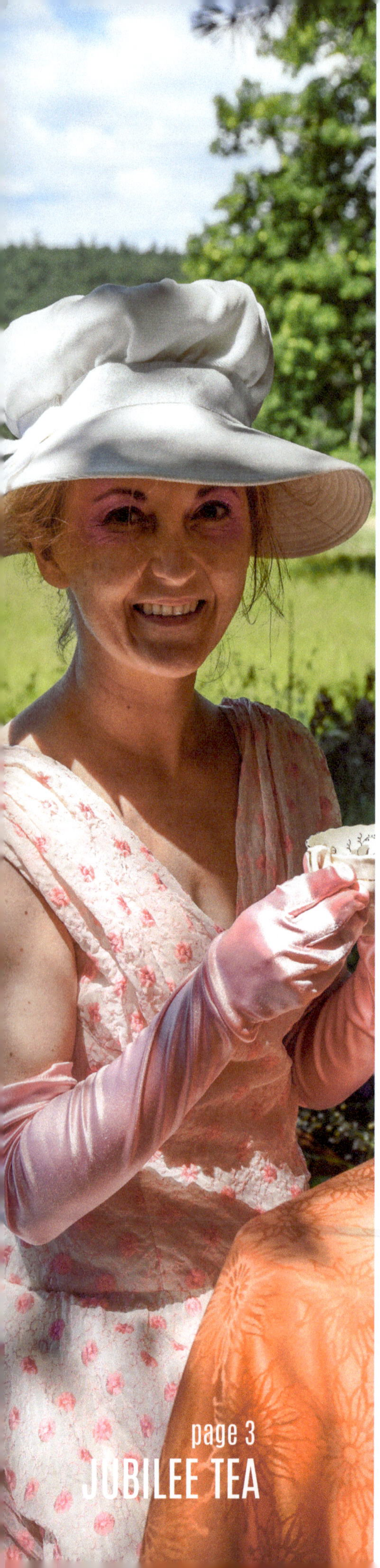

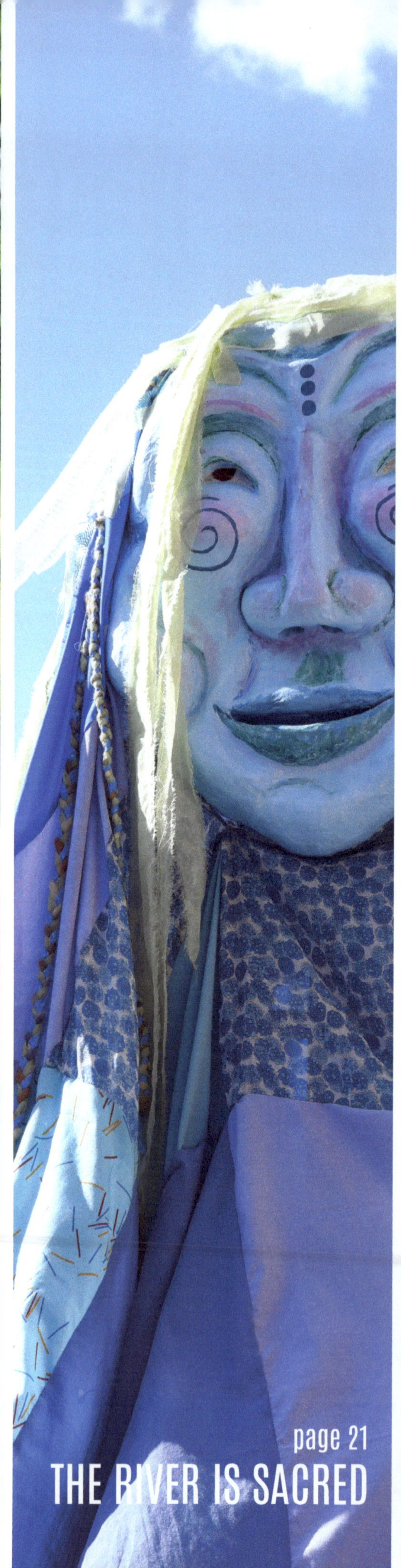

page 3
JUBILEE TEA

page 21
THE RIVER IS SACRED

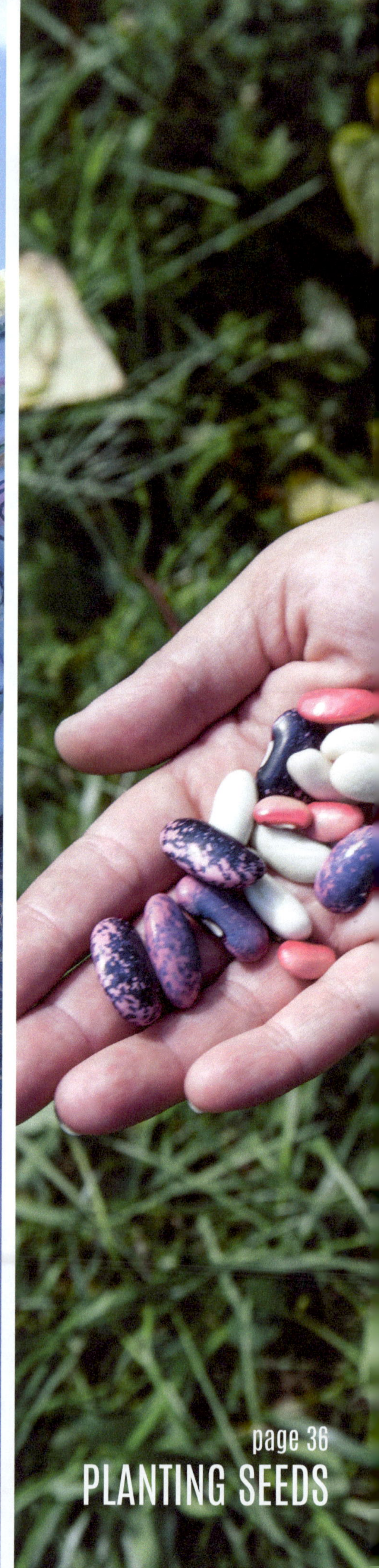

page 36
PLANTING SEEDS

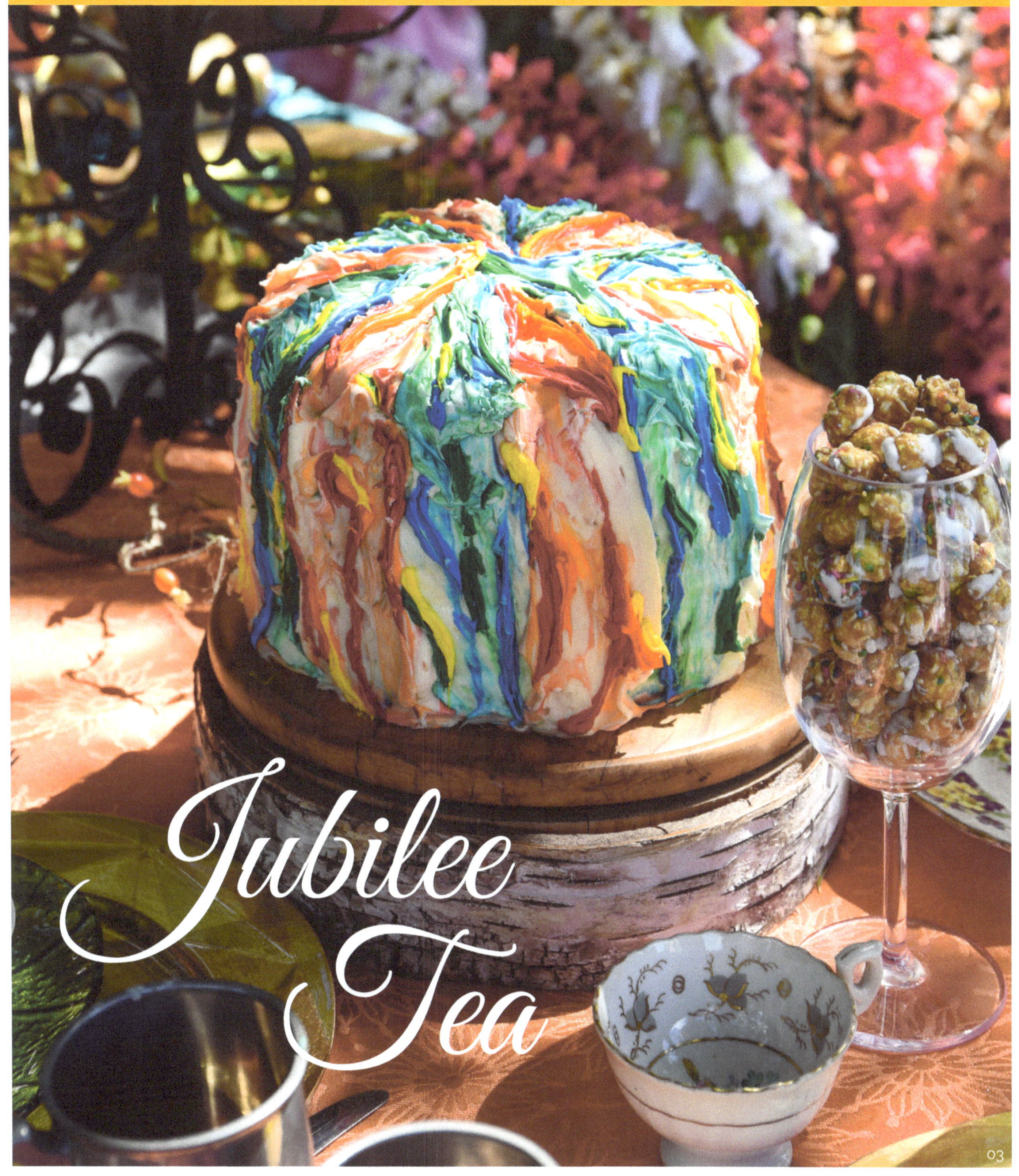

Jubilee Tea

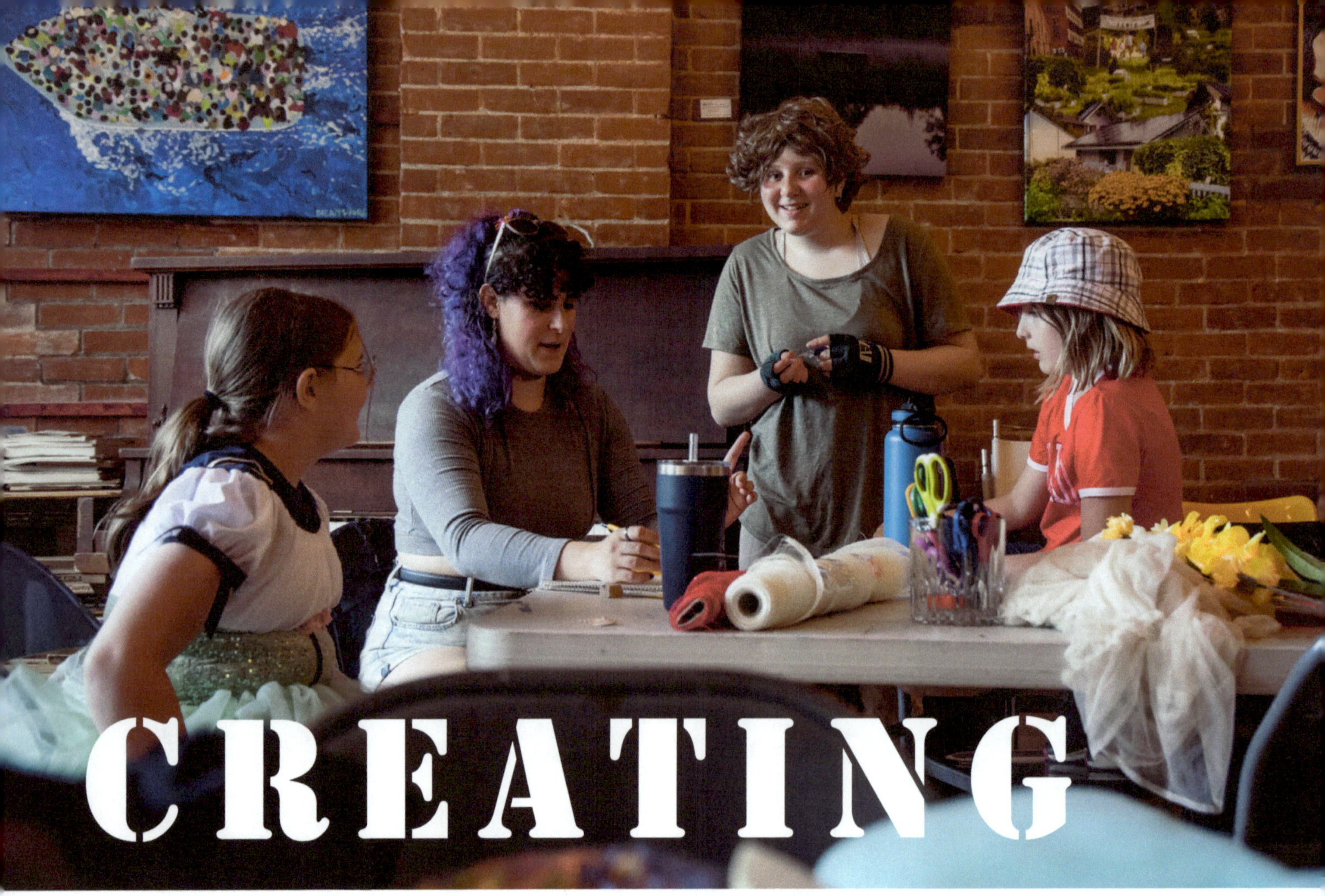

CREATING

BEHIND THE SCENES

Jubilee Tea is a short film capturing a special event to commemorate the Platinum Jubilee of Queen Elizabeth II. To bring this short film to life, the actors were asked to create characters who would attend the event. The Studio Dreamshare 2021 Acting Camp had already established *The Wild Children of Rabbit Wood Treehouse* in previous works, providing us with a backdrop and an interesting narrative to our short film. All that was left was to bring the characters to life. With strong character development, the actors could improv the shoot without saying a word.

To help do this the actors were provided with a prompt and a worksheet:

"A fantasy-like people in a solarpunk future send out an invitation to anyone who will listen. An invitation to a tea party—deep within the Northern Rabbit Woods—to help celebrate the prosperity of their lands and to offer a hand in aid to those who need it."

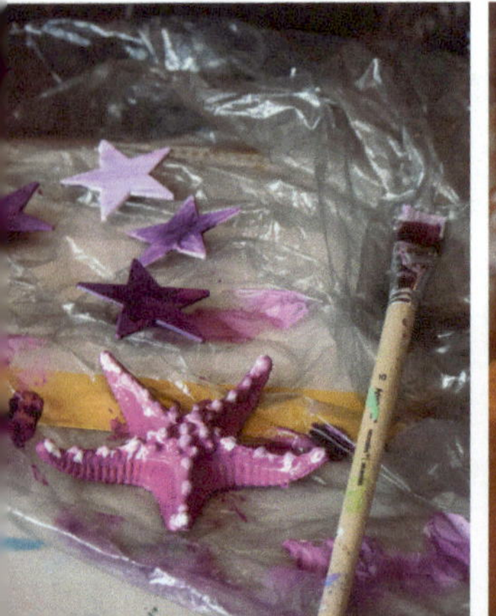
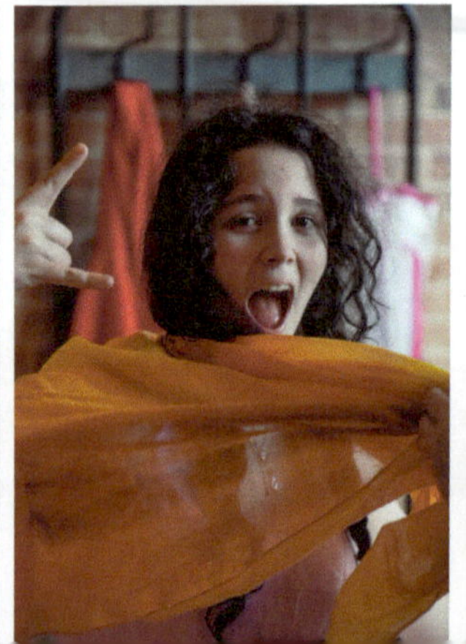
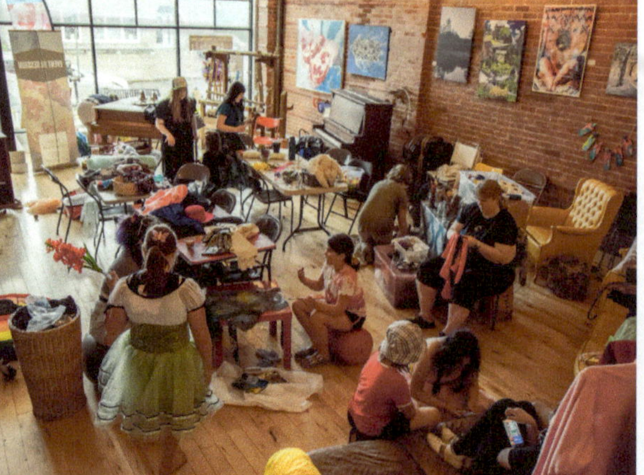
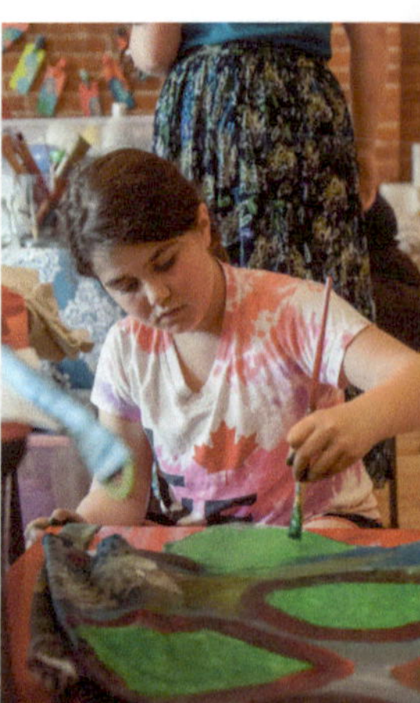

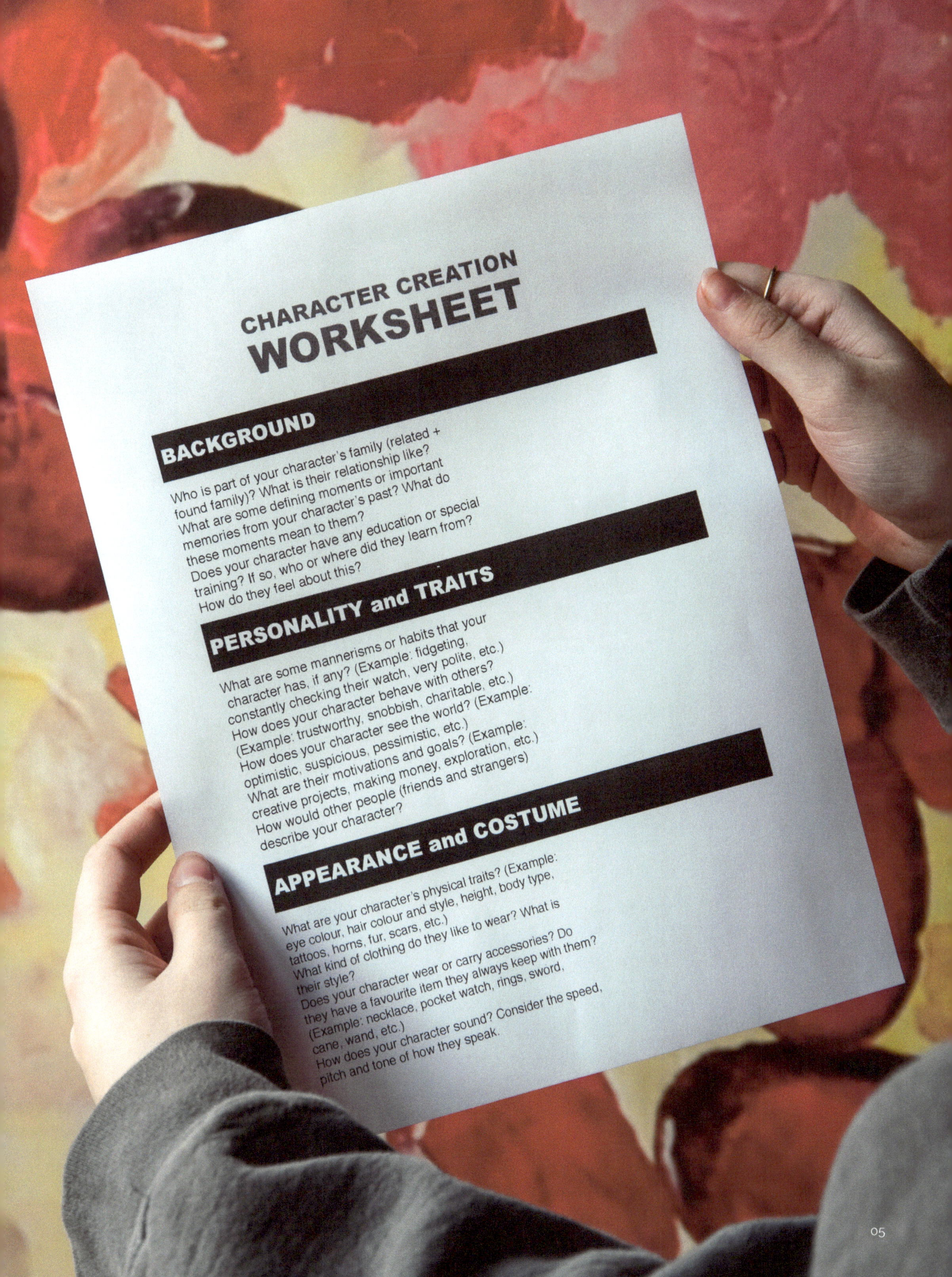
CHARACTER CREATION
WORKSHEET

BACKGROUND
Who is part of your character's family (related + found family)? What is their relationship like?
What are some defining moments or important memories from your character's past? What do these moments mean to them?
Does your character have any education or special training? If so, who or where did they learn from? How do they feel about this?

PERSONALITY and TRAITS
What are some mannerisms or habits that your character has, if any? (Example: fidgeting, constantly checking their watch, very polite, etc.)
How does your character behave with others? (Example: trustworthy, snobbish, charitable, etc.)
How does your character see the world? (Example: optimistic, suspicious, pessimistic, etc.)
What are their motivations and goals? (Example: creative projects, making money, exploration, etc.)
How would other people (friends and strangers) describe your character?

APPEARANCE and COSTUME
What are your character's physical traits? (Example: eye colour and style, height, body type, tattoos, horns, fur, scars, etc.)
What kind of clothing do they like to wear? What is their style?
Does your character wear or carry accessories? Do they have a favourite item they always keep with them? (Example: necklace, pocket watch, rings, sword, cane, wand, etc.)
How does your character sound? Consider the speed, pitch and tone of how they speak.

Jane (she/her)

FANTASY ELF

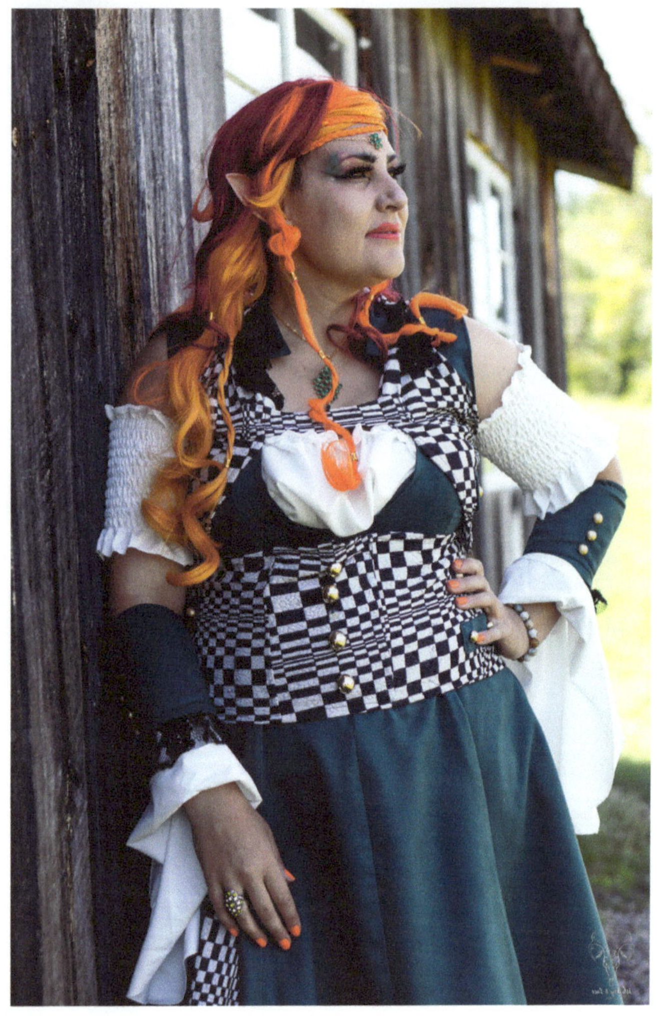

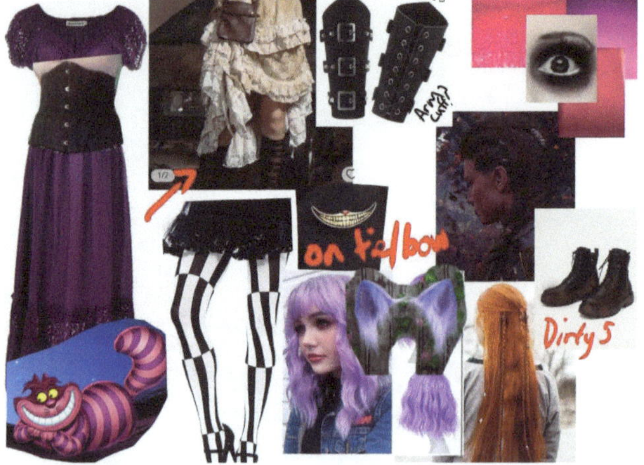

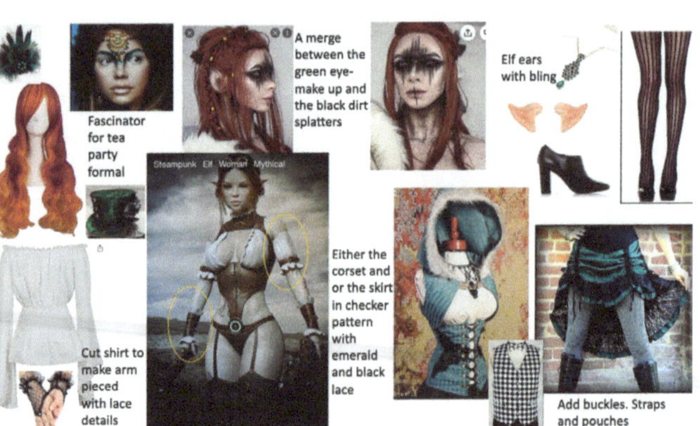

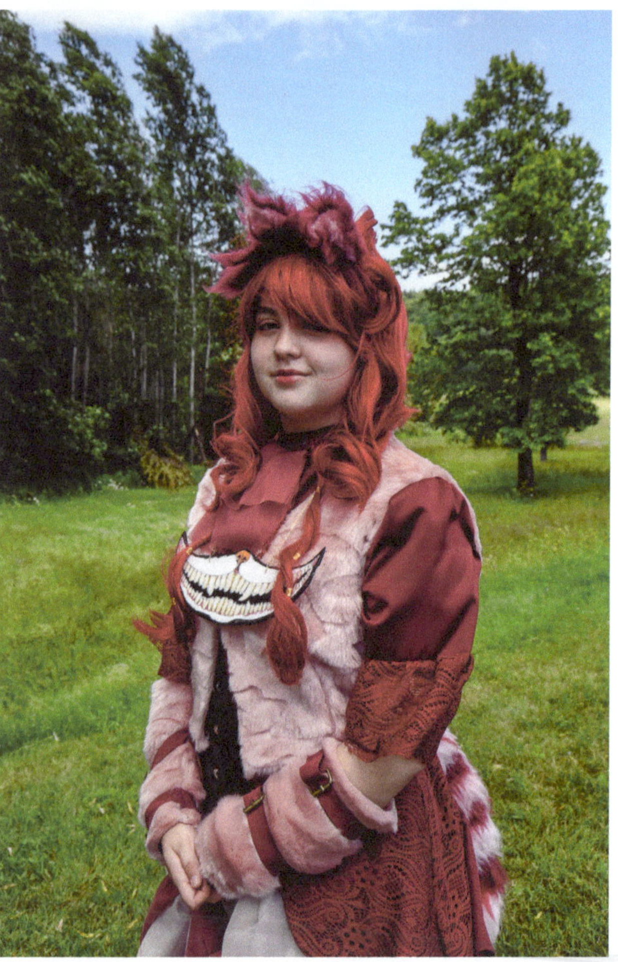

CHESHIRE CAT

Ainsley (she/her)

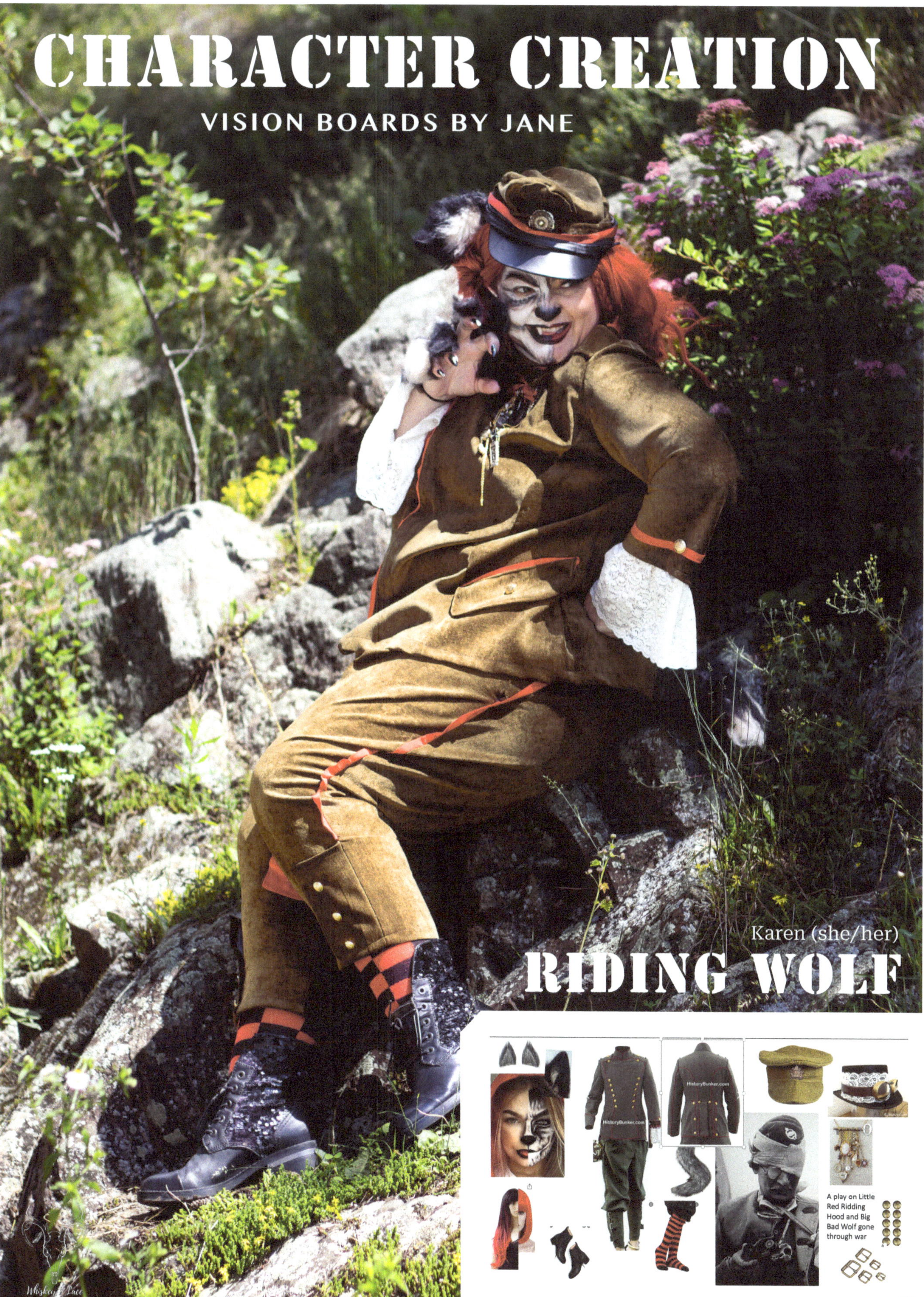

Karen (she/her)
RIDING WOLF
HistoryBunker.com
HistoryBunker.com
A play on Little
Red Ridding
Hood and Big
Bad Wolf gone
through war
Whiskey & Lace

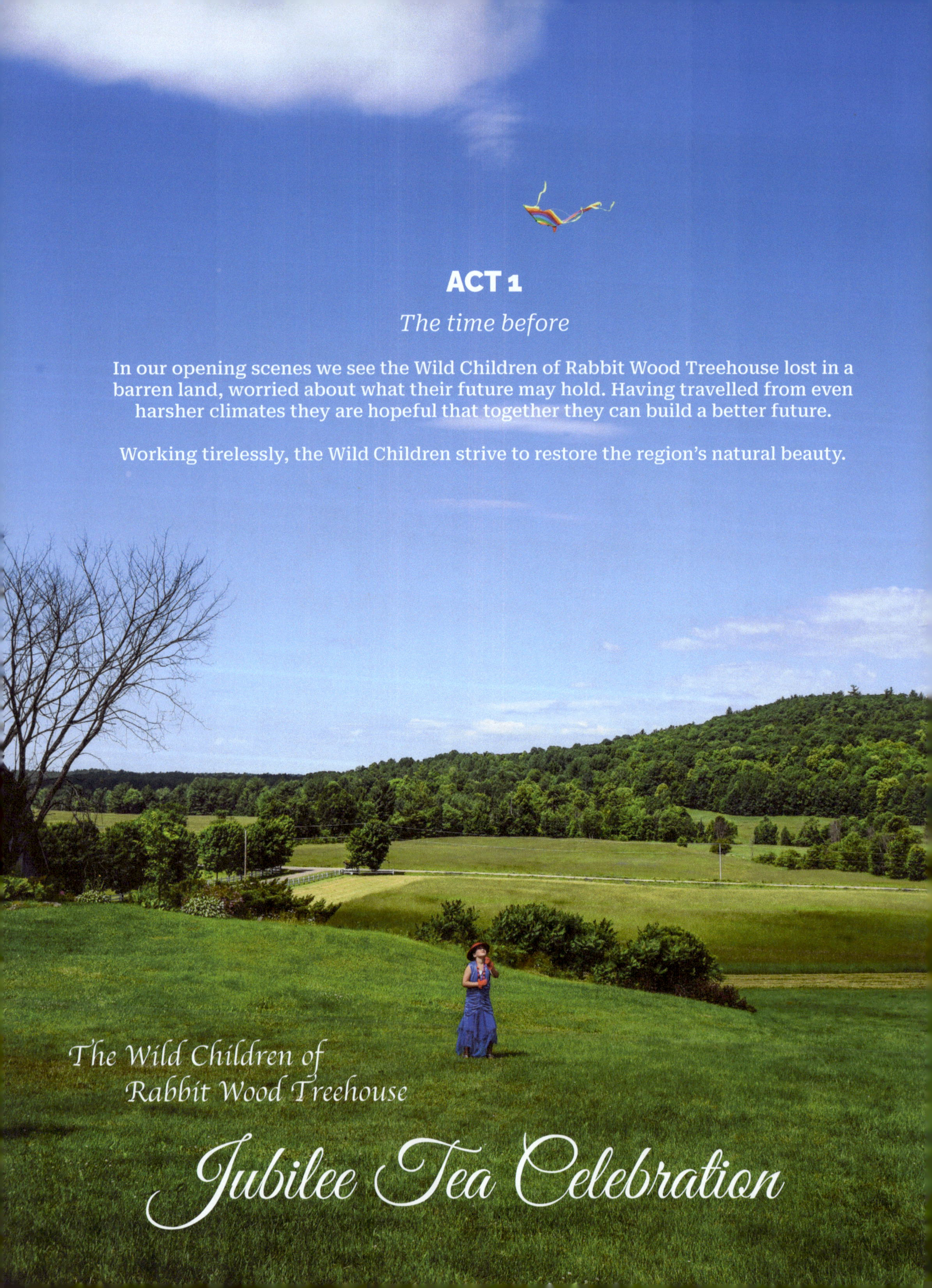

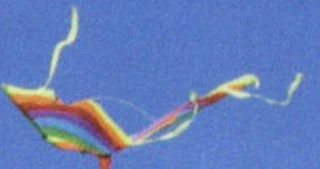

ACT 1

The time before

In our opening scenes we see the Wild Children of Rabbit Wood Treehouse lost in a barren land, worried about what their future may hold. Having travelled from even harsher climates they are hopeful that together they can build a better future.

Working tirelessly, the Wild Children strive to restore the region's natural beauty.

*The Wild Children of
Rabbit Wood Treehouse*

Jubilee Tea Celebration

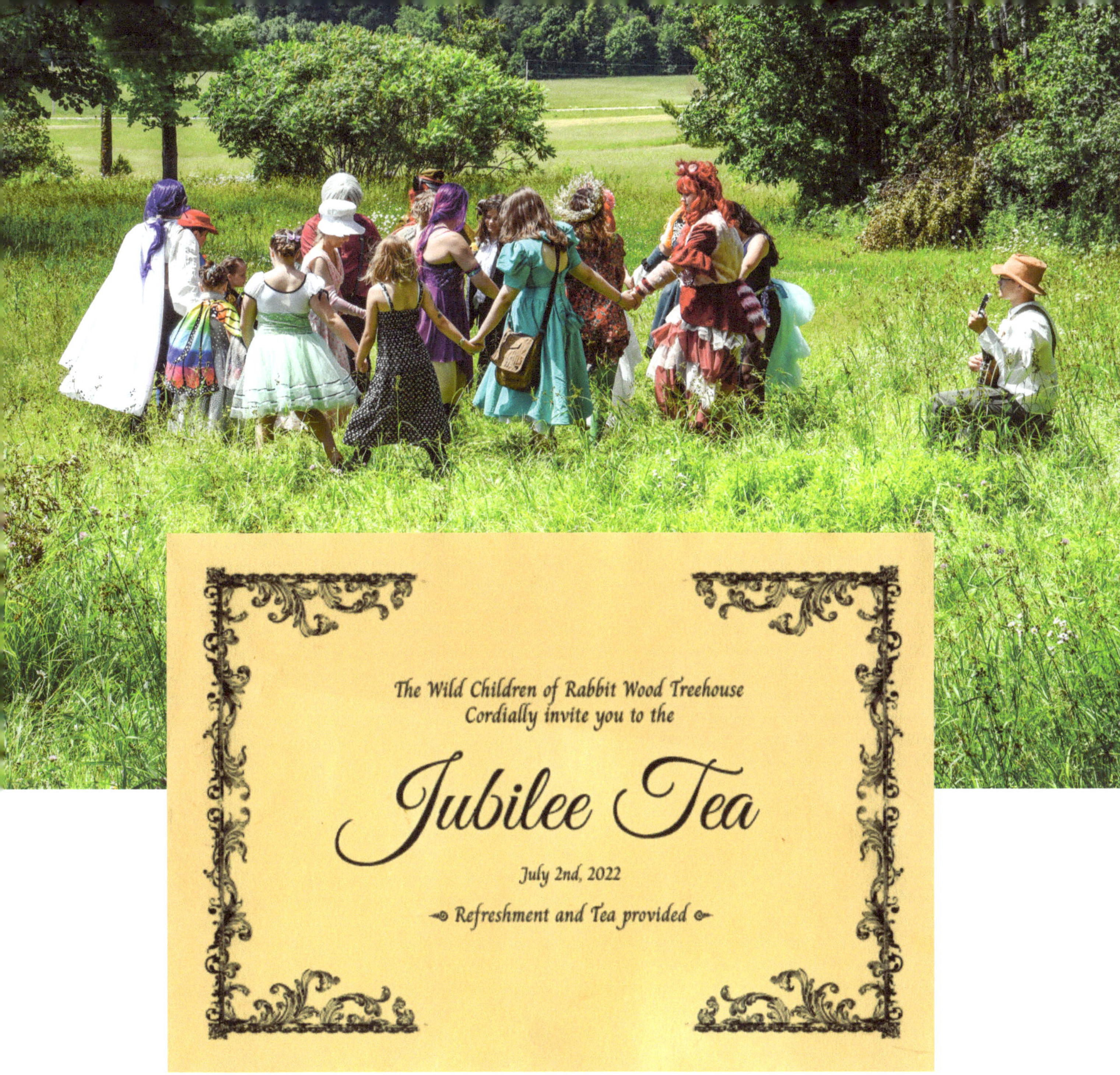

ACT 2

It's time for a celebration

Having spent decades working to improve the land, the Wild Children decide it is time to open themselves up to the outside world. The Wild Children send out beautifully-crafted invitations across the cosmos, hoping to attract a diverse crowd of wonderful people. Their efforts were not in vain as people from far and wide answered the call.

The preparations are set and the entertainers are ready:
The Jubilee Tea Celebration is about to begin.

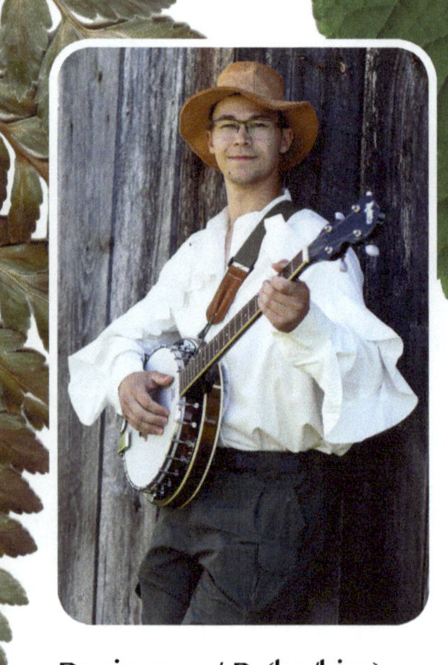

Banjoman / R (he/him)
A special guest of the Wild Children of Rabbit Wood Treehouse, invited for his musical talents. Thanks to his magic banjo he is able to play a whole orchestra's worth of music at once.

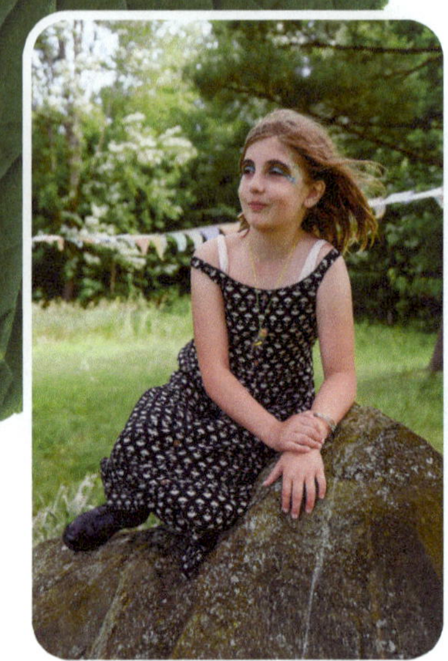

Hyacinth Trinket/ Madeline (she/her)
Having always had a perceptive mind, Hyacinth has spent much of her life unravelling the mysteries that surround her. Armed with a notebook and pen she excitingly attends the party, curious about what she could learn from the Rabbit Wood folk.

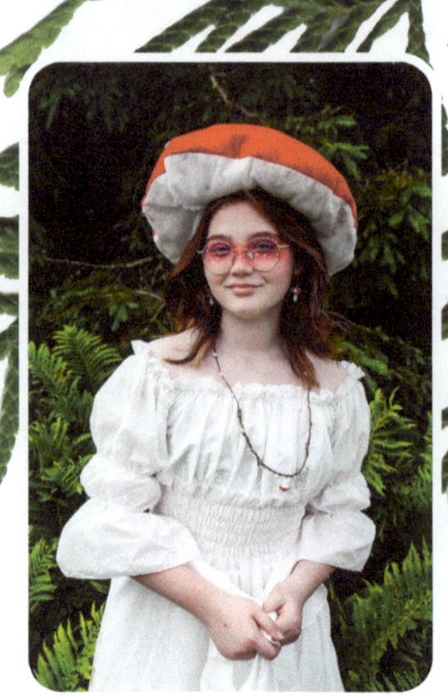

Miya /Eva (she/her)
A mushroom girl from the neighbouring woods was thrilled to hear the Wild Children of Rabbit Wood Treehouse would be hosting such a lavish celebration. Seeing Leaf skeptical of their surroundings, she offered to show her the ropes on how to find joy.

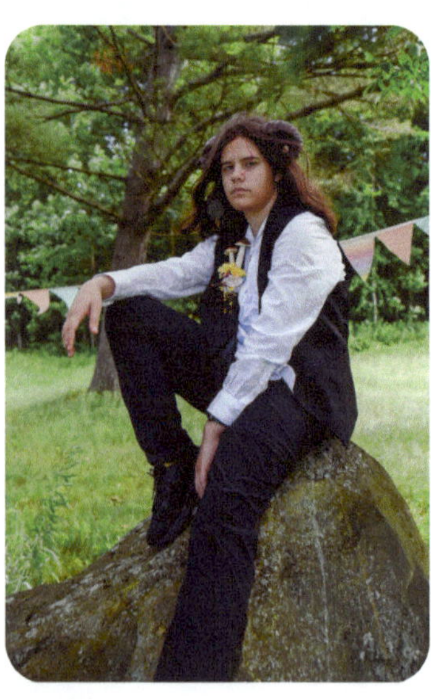

Leaf / Ella (she/her)
Having grown up in hardship, Leaf turned to a life of crime to get by. As an assassin for hire she grew a very thick shell trusting very few people. A concerned friend saw the announcement for the Jubilee Tea and knew it was time for a change. Set up with a fake assassination job, Leaf was sent out to the party. Upon arrival she was so mesmerized by the camaraderie that she discarded her contract and joined in the revelry.

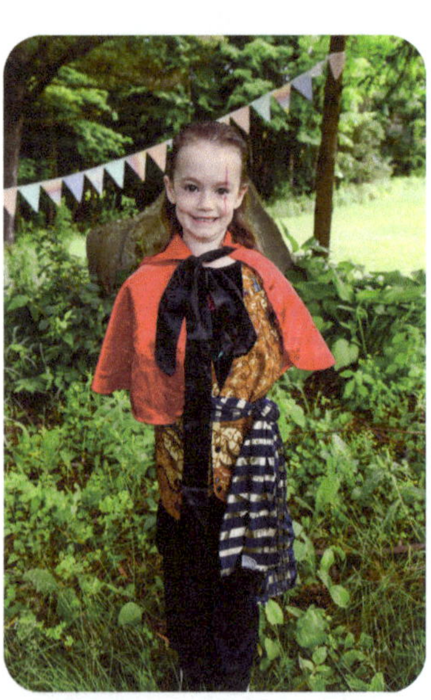

Matilda / Audrey (she/her)
Having a rough past and a harsh attitude has helped First Mate Matilda on the high seas. Her specialty was stealing back lost treasure and pilfered goods, making sure they reached the people they were first taken from. Now, however, she seeks to gain more allies in the never-ending battle against evil and has turned to the Wild Children of Rabbit Wood Treehouse for aid, hoping that these new allies can be the shift in the tide.

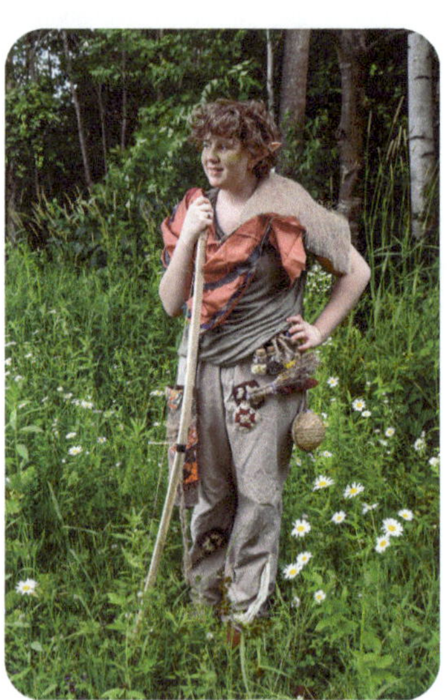

Gonnalf / Ein (they/them)
A wood elf by birth, Gonnalf has grown to become very distrusting of humans as they have often disappointed them with their neglectful actions towards nature and its animals. Skeptical at first of the tea party invitation, Gonnalf decides to give them a chance, and their skepticism turns to friendship as they learn that one of the children of Rabbit Wood treehouse has learned sign language to help ease communications.

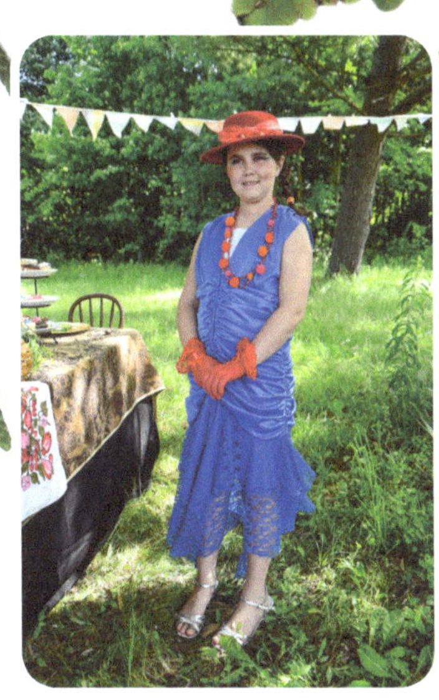

Daisy / Josie (she/her)

A flower faerie of the Rabbit Woods, Daisy is a friend of the Wild Children and has eagerly awaited the day of the celebration. She is ready to dance and frolic the day away.

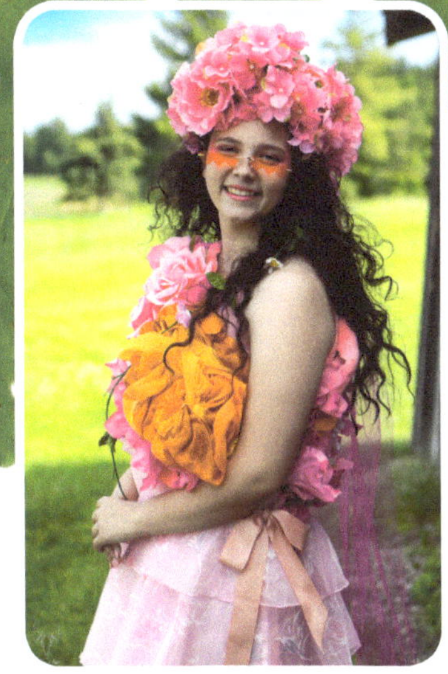

Skull / Bren (they/them)

A flower faerie of the Rabbit Woods, Skull is one of the first to RSVP their attendance to the tea party. They spend most of their time at the event dancing in bliss surrounded by such joyfulness.

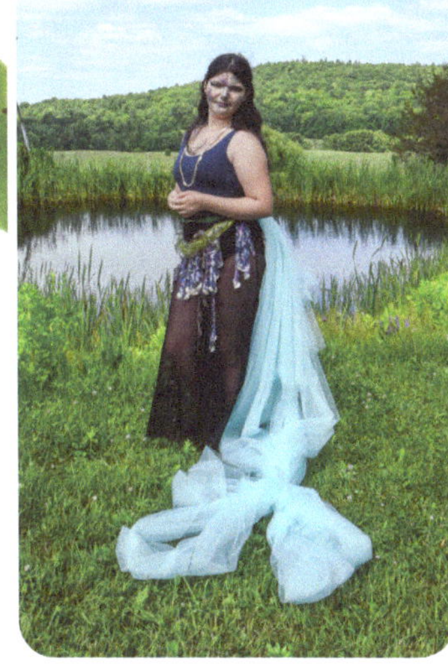

Aqua / Clare (she/her)

A river mermaid, Aqua was intrigued by the notion of Rabbit Wood treehouse hosting a tea party. Although often choosing to enjoy nature in its quiet stillness, she chooses to attend the celebration and is excited by this grand gesture of camaraderie.

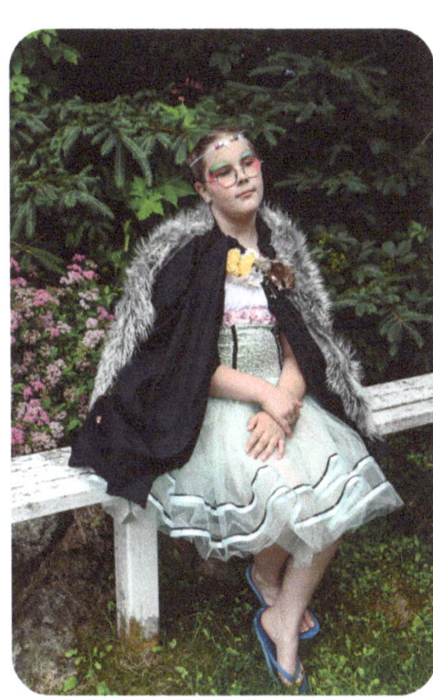

Artemis / Gwen (she/her)

A member of the Wild Children, Artemis is thrilled to finally be hosting the Jubilee Tea where all those who nurture nature are welcomed. She has prepared diligently—even learning foreign languages to help ease communications—in the hopes of bolstering the Wild Children's ranks. She remains hopeful that they may retake more of the lost lands for nature.

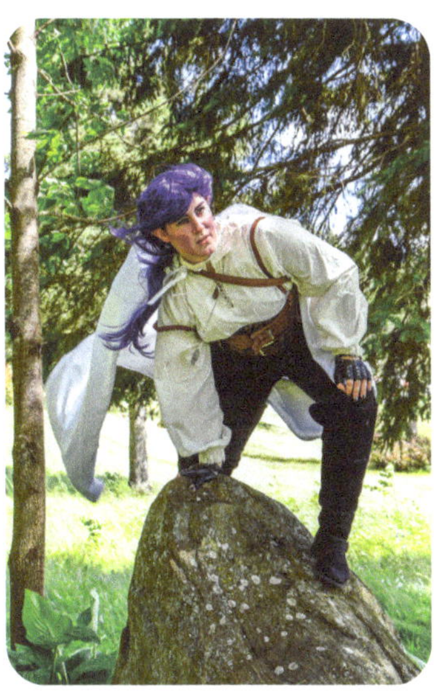

Kit / Siren (any pronouns)

A special guest of The Wild Children of Rabbit Wood Treehouse, Kit was invited for his connections to the neighbouring realms. A being imbued with wild celestial magic, Kit is often very busy travelling the realms providing aid to those in need. Kit looks forward to sharing the stories from today's event with whomever they meet on their travels.

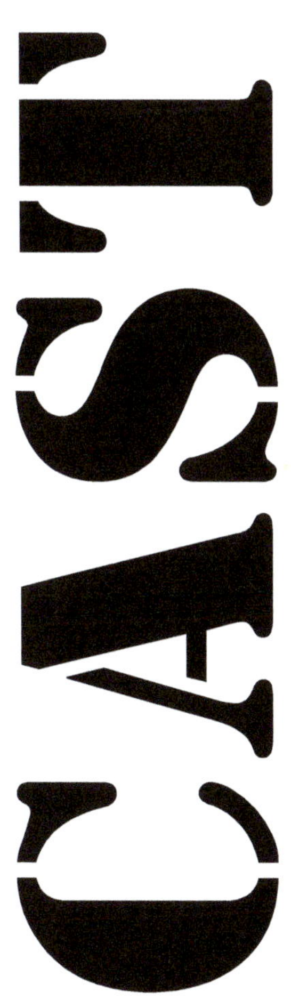

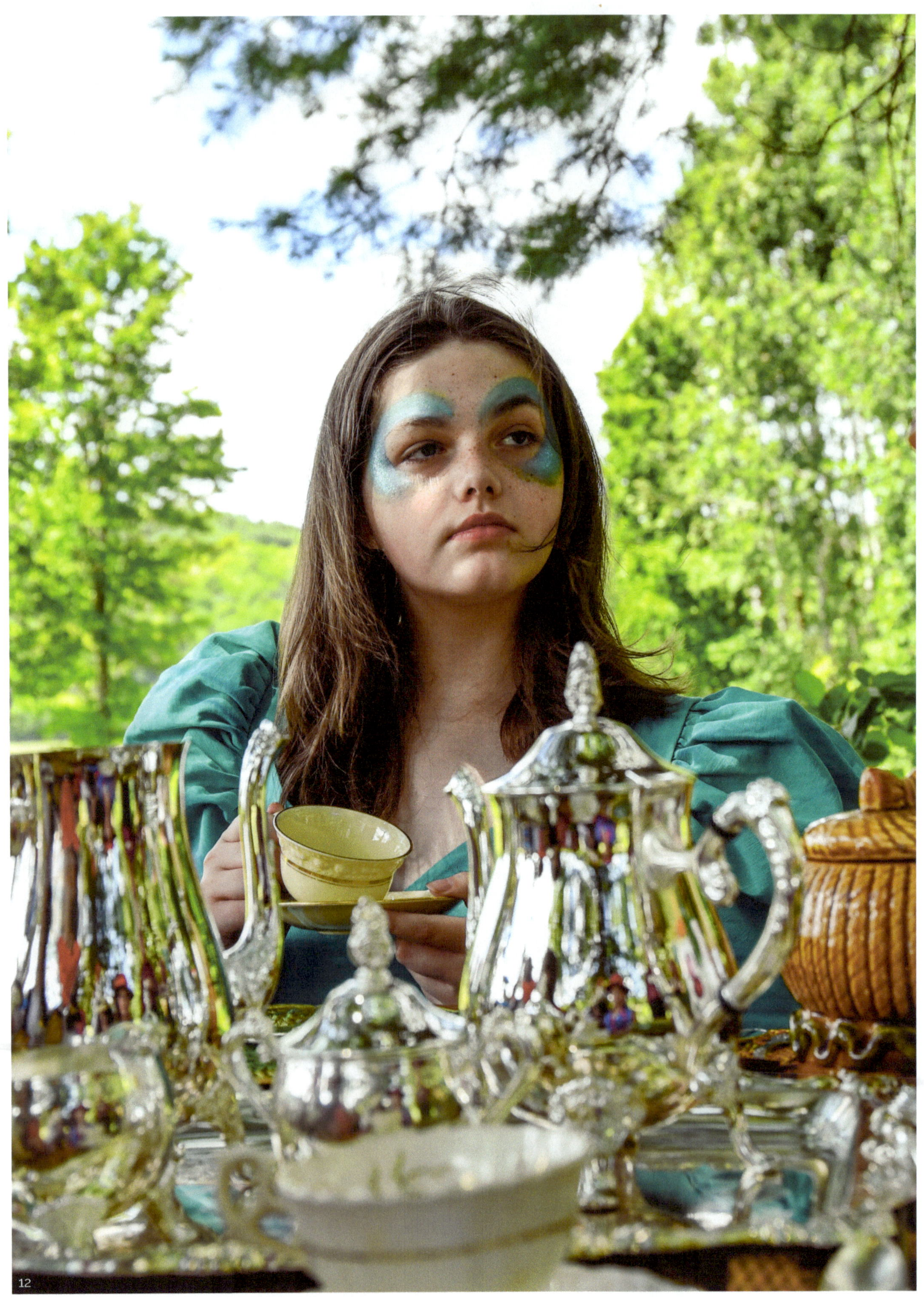

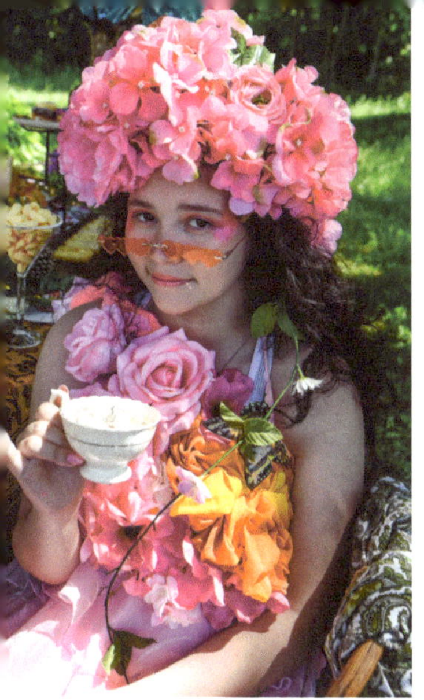
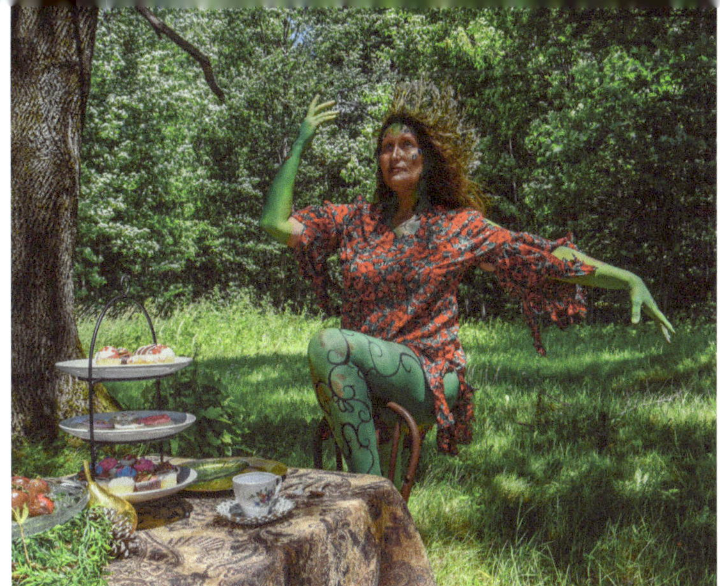
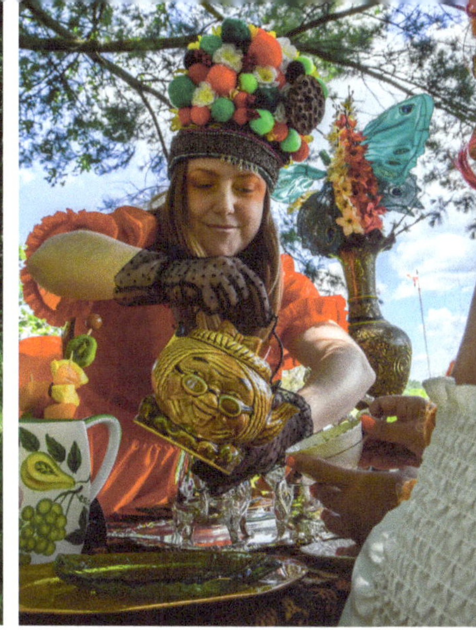

ACT 3

We have guests

The varied guests arrive and the celebration goes off without a hitch. It seems there is something for everyone as the crowds are mesmerized by the entertainers, swept away by the music or smile softly with full bellies. As the guests depart, everyone agrees: this is an event that will be talked about for generations.

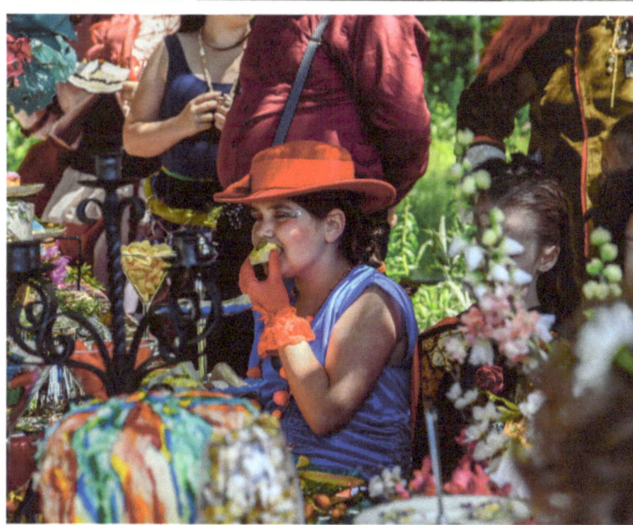
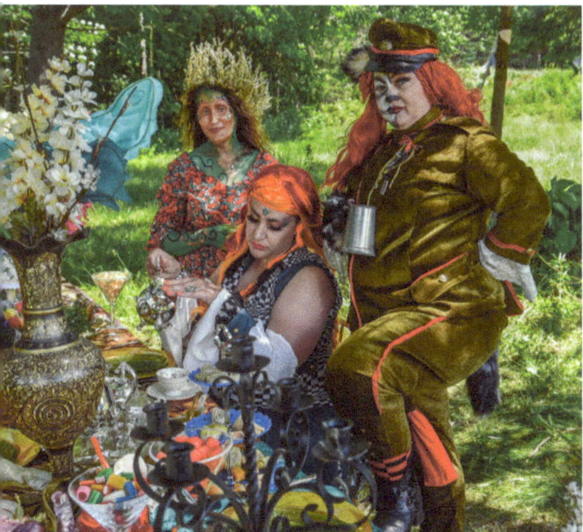
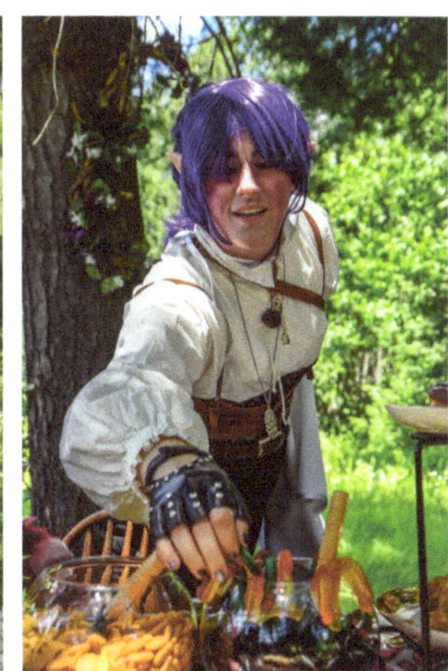
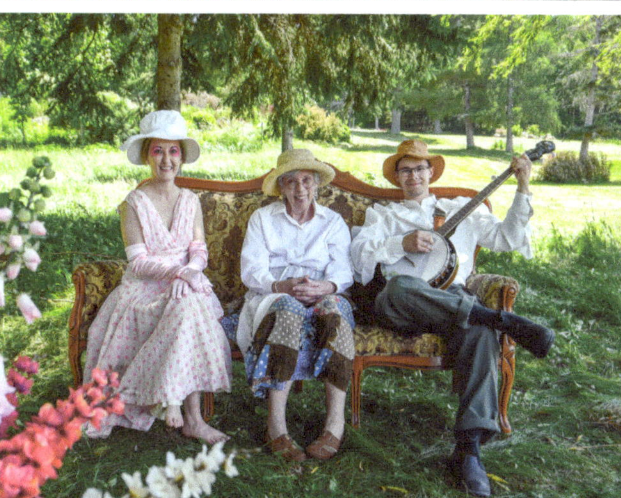
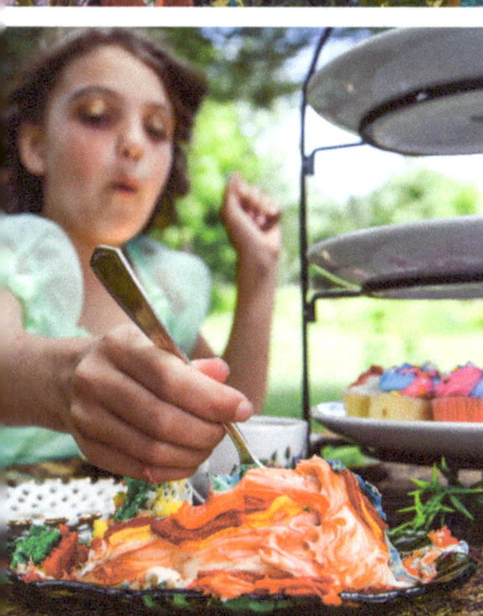
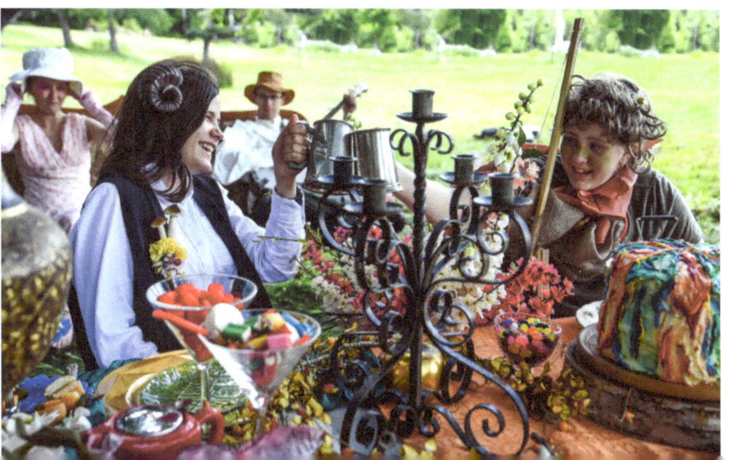
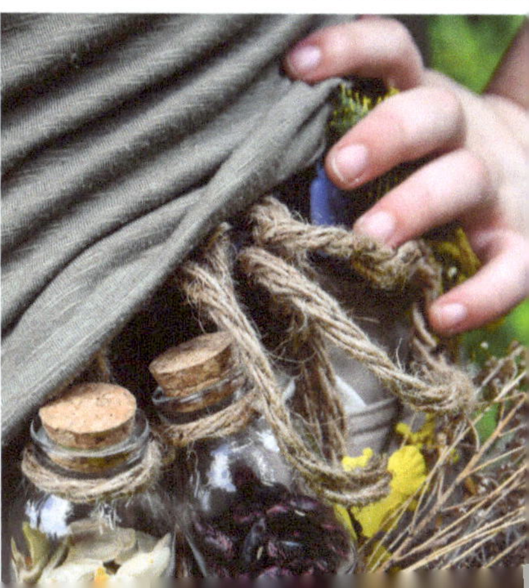

QUEEN CONNECTIONS

The parents of Ottawa Valley resident Margaret Phillips both served in World War II with the British military; her mother, Marie Patricia Phillips, was with the Women's Auxiliary Air Force, and her father, William Frayne Phillips was a pilot with the Royal Air Force. Her father continued to serve in the diplomatic corps long after the war, and the family resided in apartments with other service members, all of whom were invited to a garden tea party for Queen Elizabeth II on July 21, 1954. The dress worn by Marie Phillips on that special occasion found new life 68 years later when Natascha Bourgault donned it for the role of Marie Patricia Phillips in the film, this time at a garden tea party that was part of celebrations for the Queen's Platinum Jubilee in 2022.

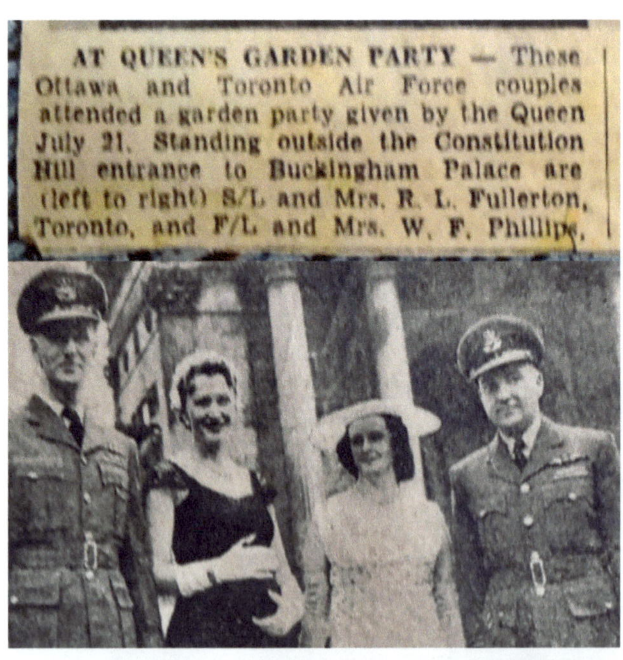

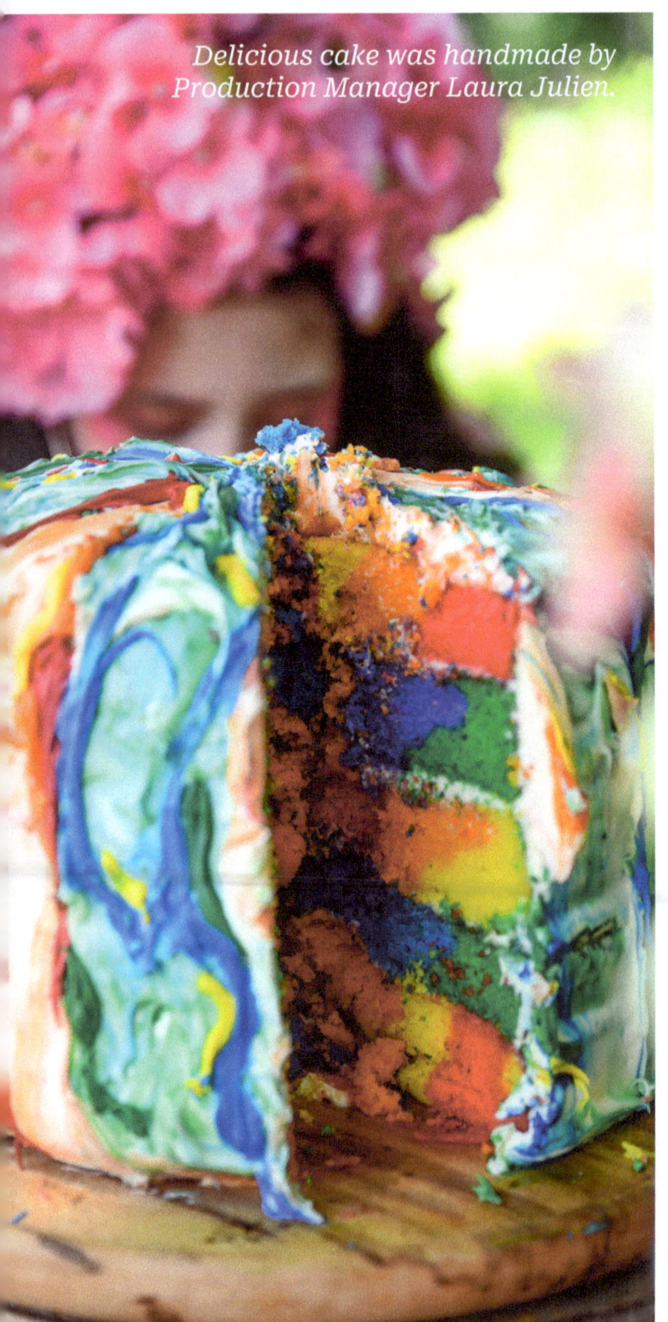

Delicious cake was handmade by Production Manager Laura Julien.

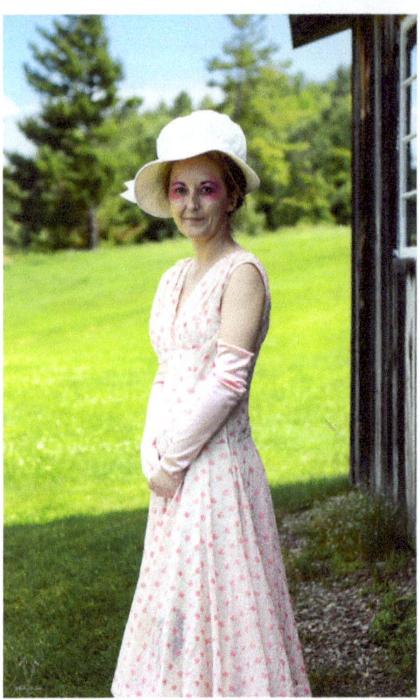

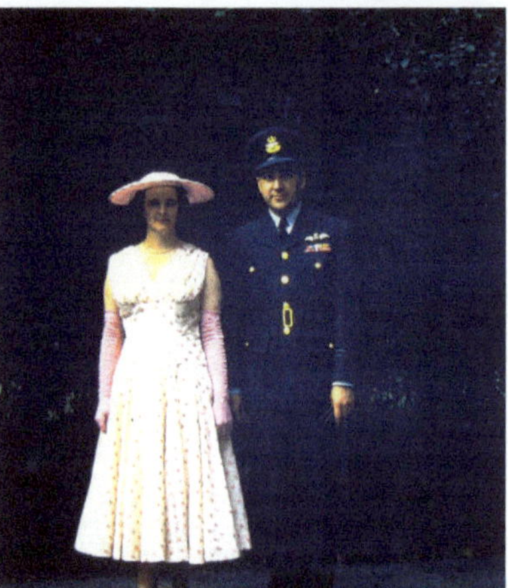

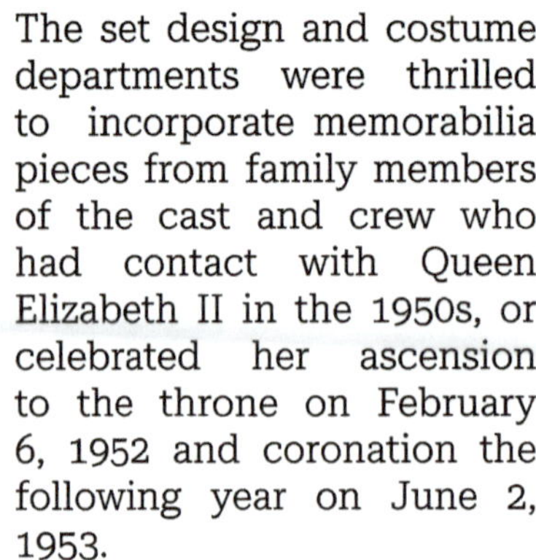

The set design and costume departments were thrilled to incorporate memorabilia pieces from family members of the cast and crew who had contact with Queen Elizabeth II in the 1950s, or celebrated her ascension to the throne on February 6, 1952 and coronation the following year on June 2, 1953.

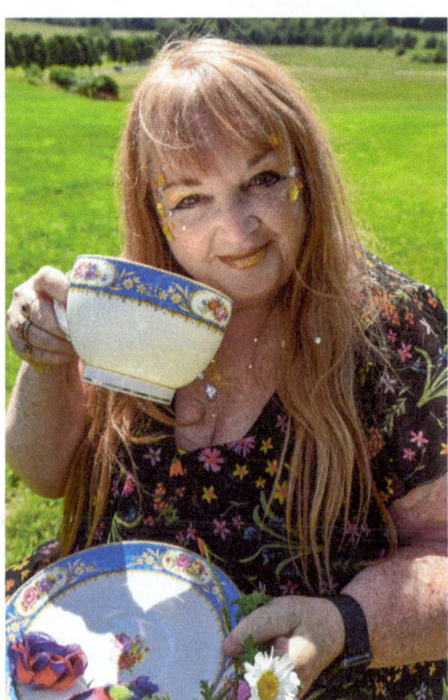

Margaret Phillips

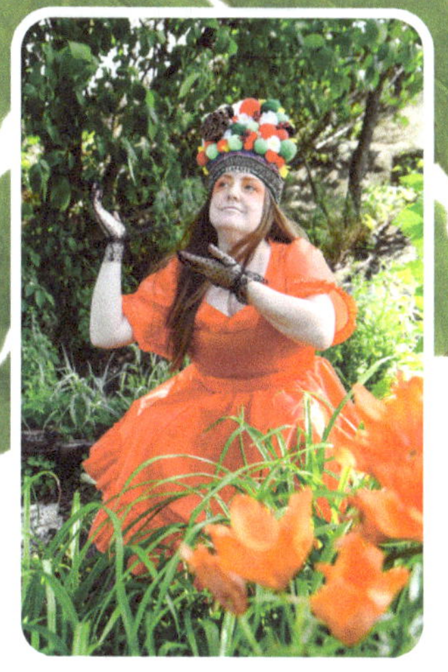

Monarch Butterfly /
Dreamshare
(they/them)

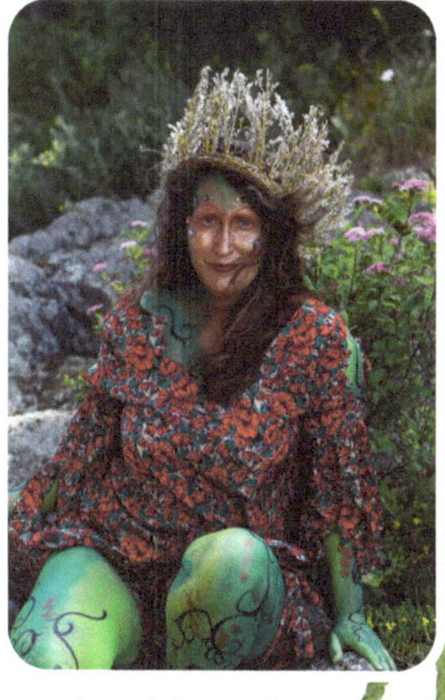

Earth Spirit / Kristen
(she/her)

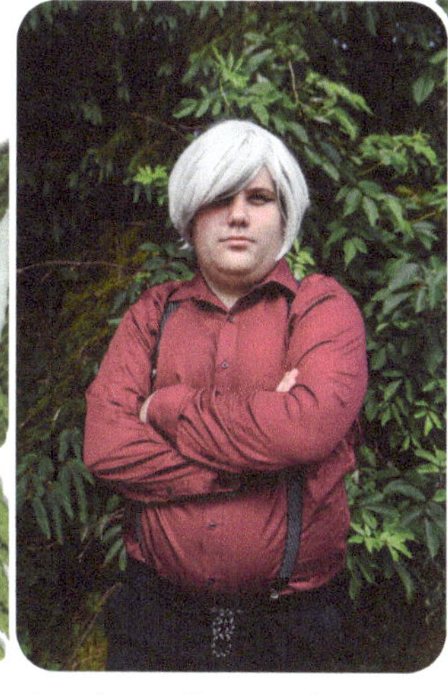

Oswin Hyjinx / Ash
(they/them)

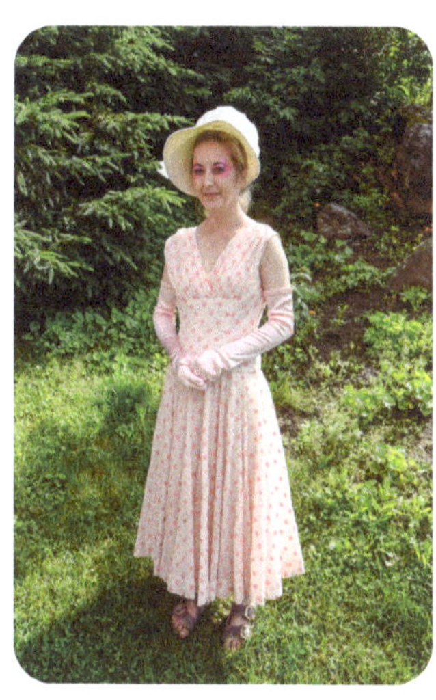

Marie Patricia Phillips /
Natascha (she/her)

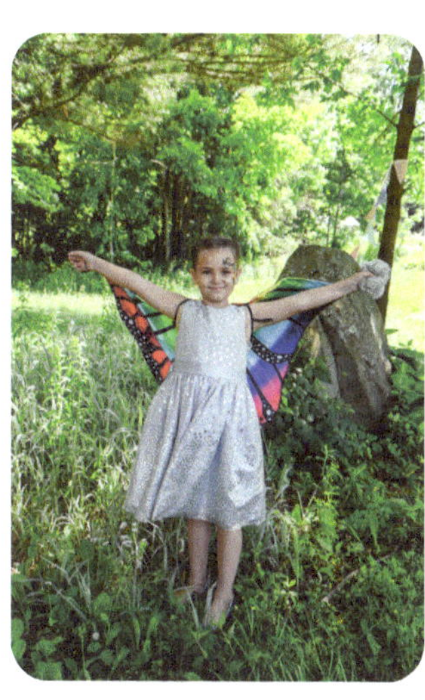

Margaret's
Granddaughter /
Rose (she/her)

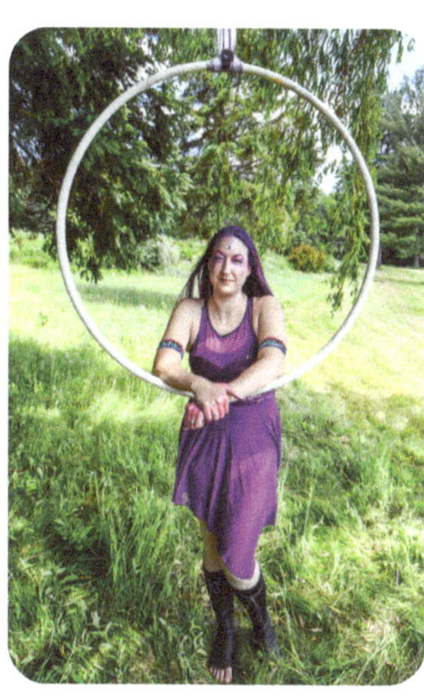

Lady Cirque /
Amber (she/her)

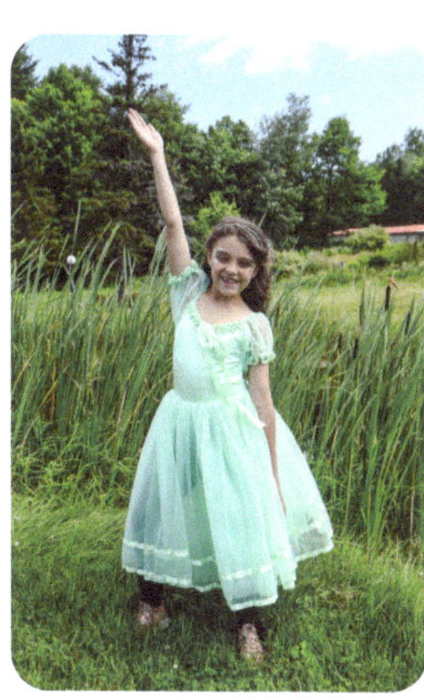

Sophia / Layla (she/her)

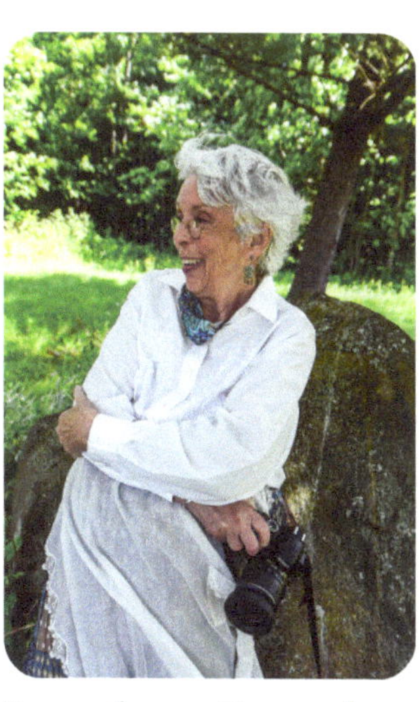

Persephone (Pursa-phone)/
Beth (she/her)

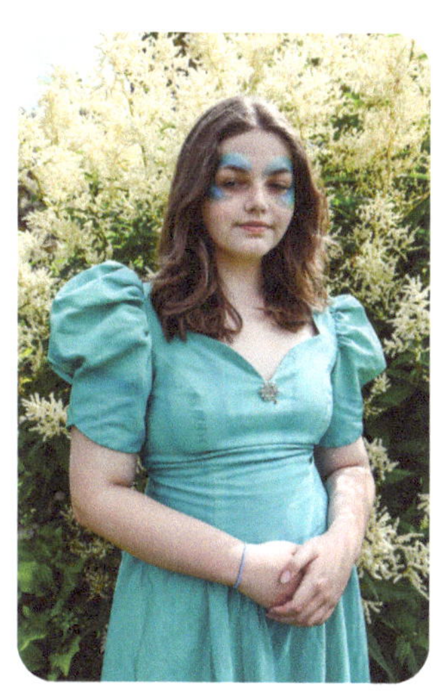

Lilith Ather /
Emma (she/her)

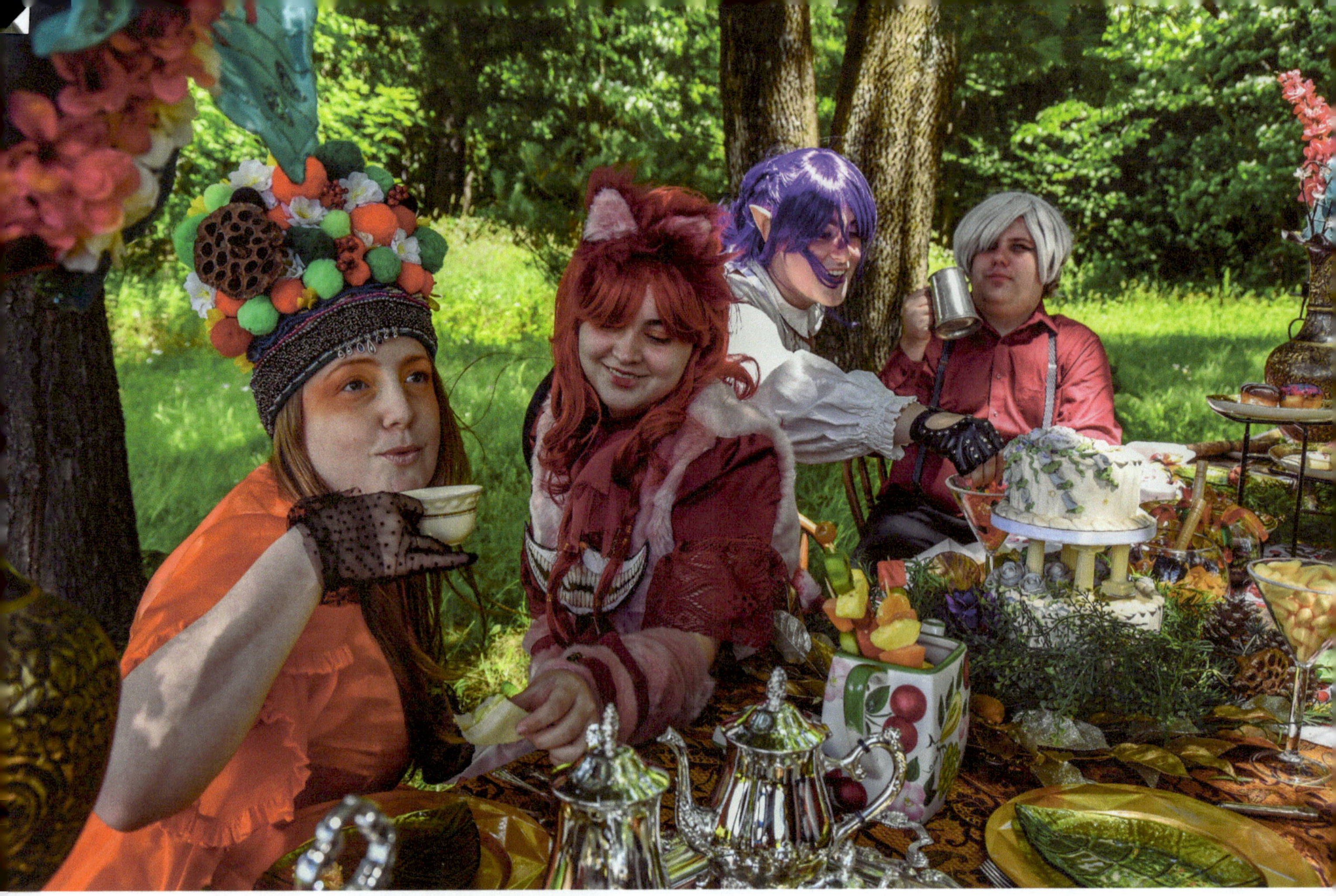

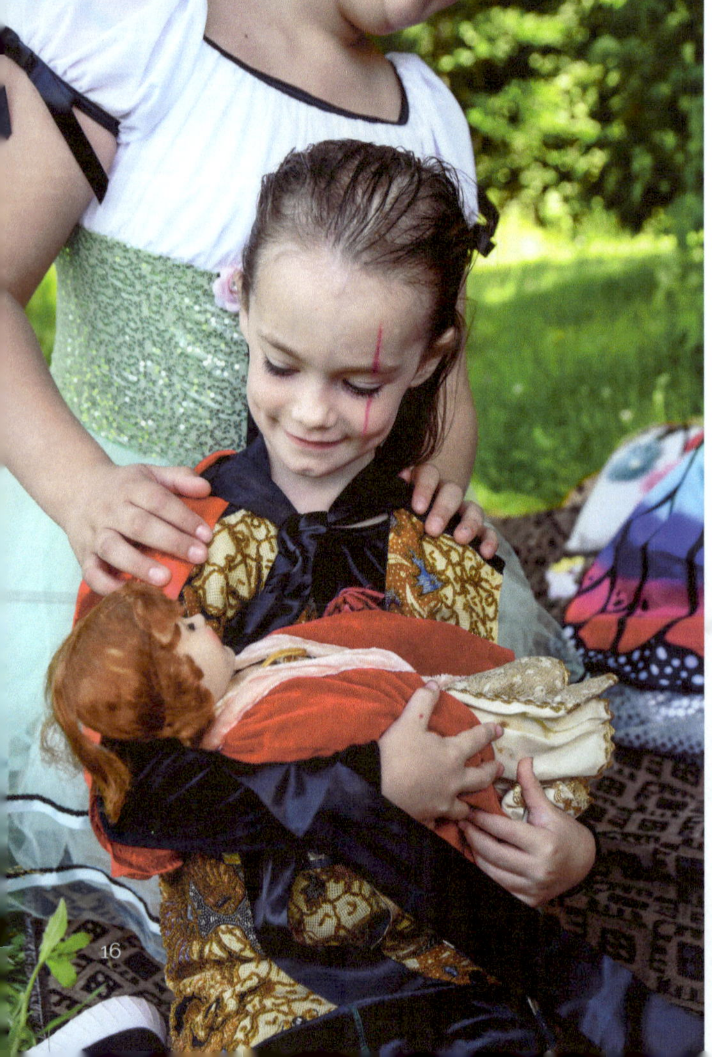

Another participant in the movie, Kristen Glowa, loaned her mother's doll for use on the set. Dale Torgerson received the doll in the early 1950s as a gift to commemorate the Queen's coronation. In 1953, Reliable Coronation Dolls in various sizes were sold to celebrate and commemorate the occasion of the Queen's coronation. The dolls were fully decorated like the Queen in her coronation robe, white satin gown with gold trim, ribbon sash with her name and tiara. The pictured 15" doll has a mark on its head: A RELIABLE DOLL.

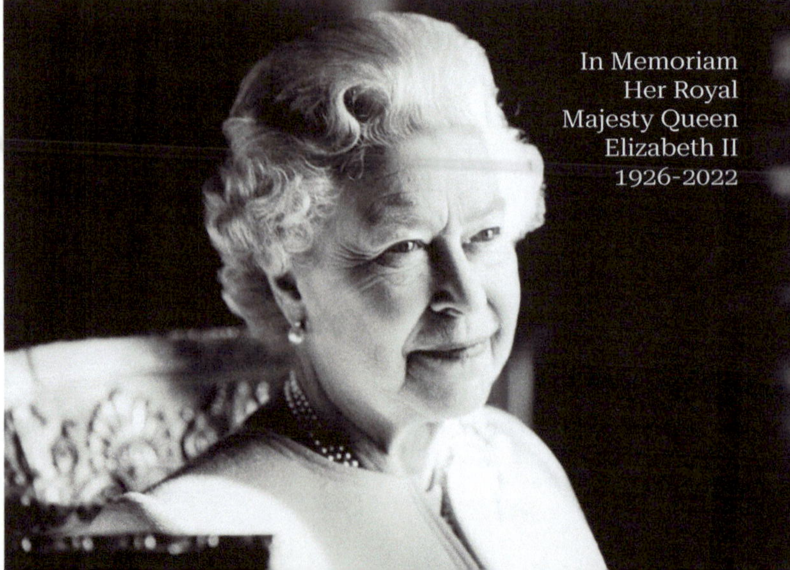

CREATIVE TEAM

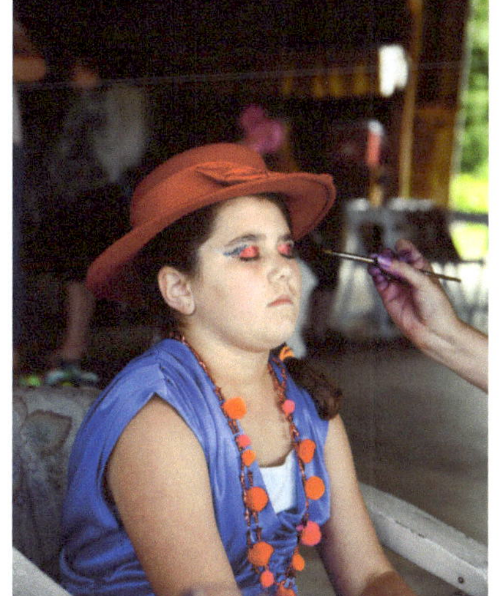
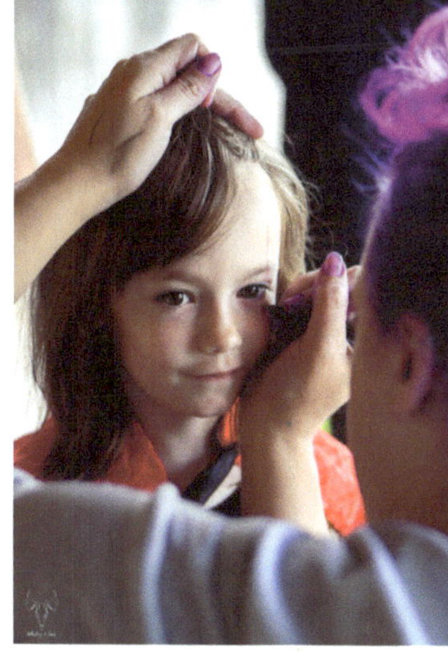

Director
Cameron Dreamshare

Executive Producer/Choreographer
Dorian Pearce

Production Manager
Laura Julien

Acting Coach
Siren Boudreau

Director of Photography
Jake Neville

Producer
Rose Bennett

Associate Producer
Tanya Leamen

Prop Master
Margaret Phillips

Costume Design
Created by each cast member

Makeup Artists
Amber Buchwald, Ainsley O'Hagan,
Margaret Phillips, Tania Crook Vocilka,
Jane Wood

Hair Stylists
Siren Boudreau, Tanya Leamen

Craft Service
Koren Julien

Still Photographers
Rose Bennett,
Rose Bennett Photography
Chantal Lambert,
Whiskey & Lace Boudoir Photography

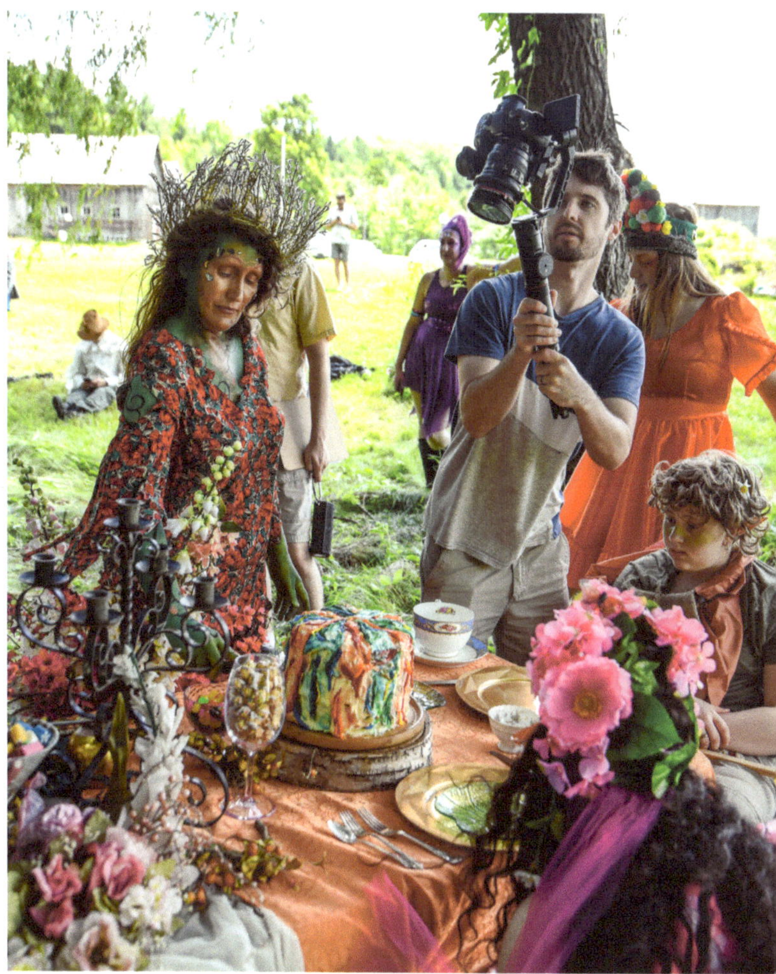
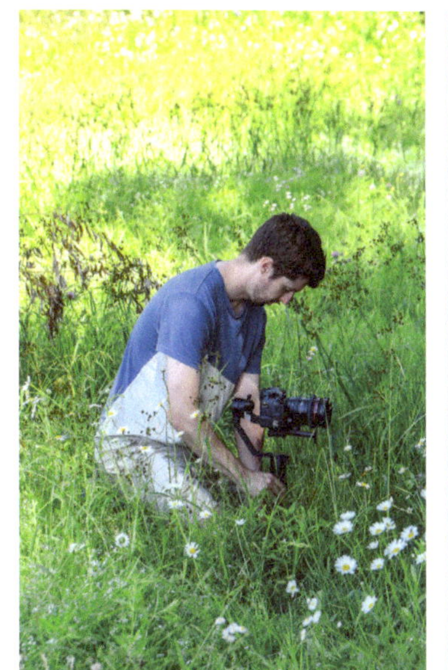
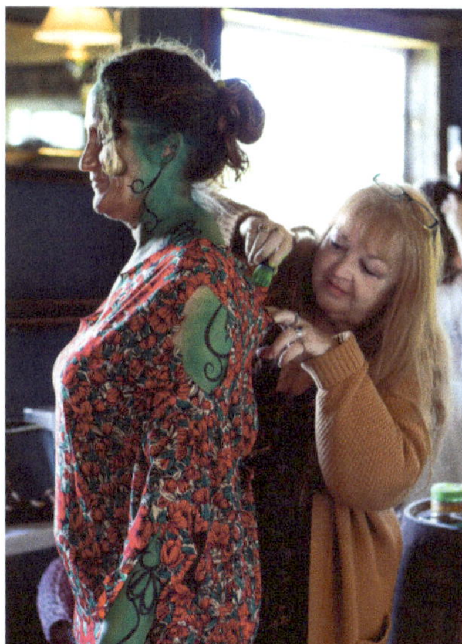

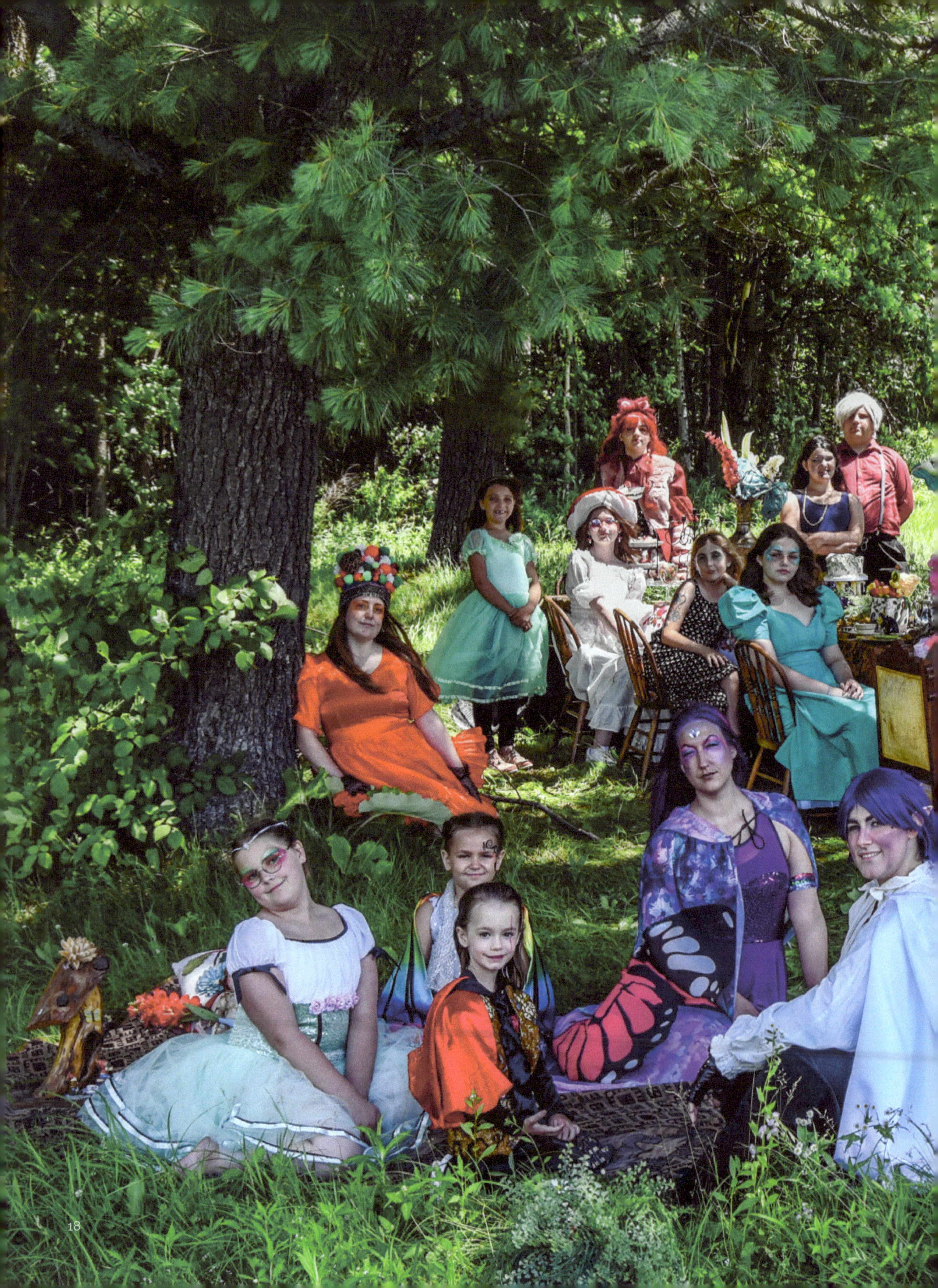

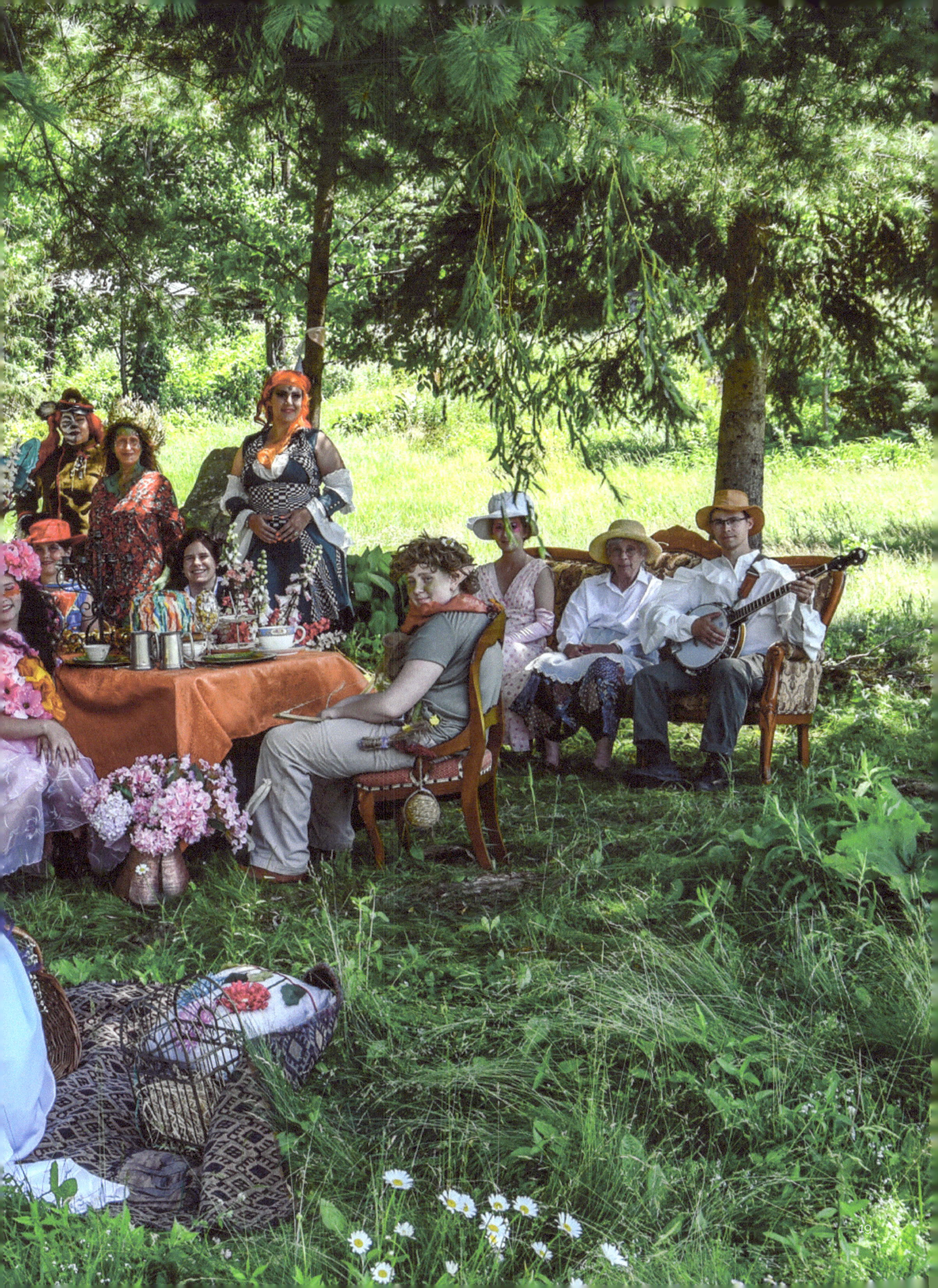

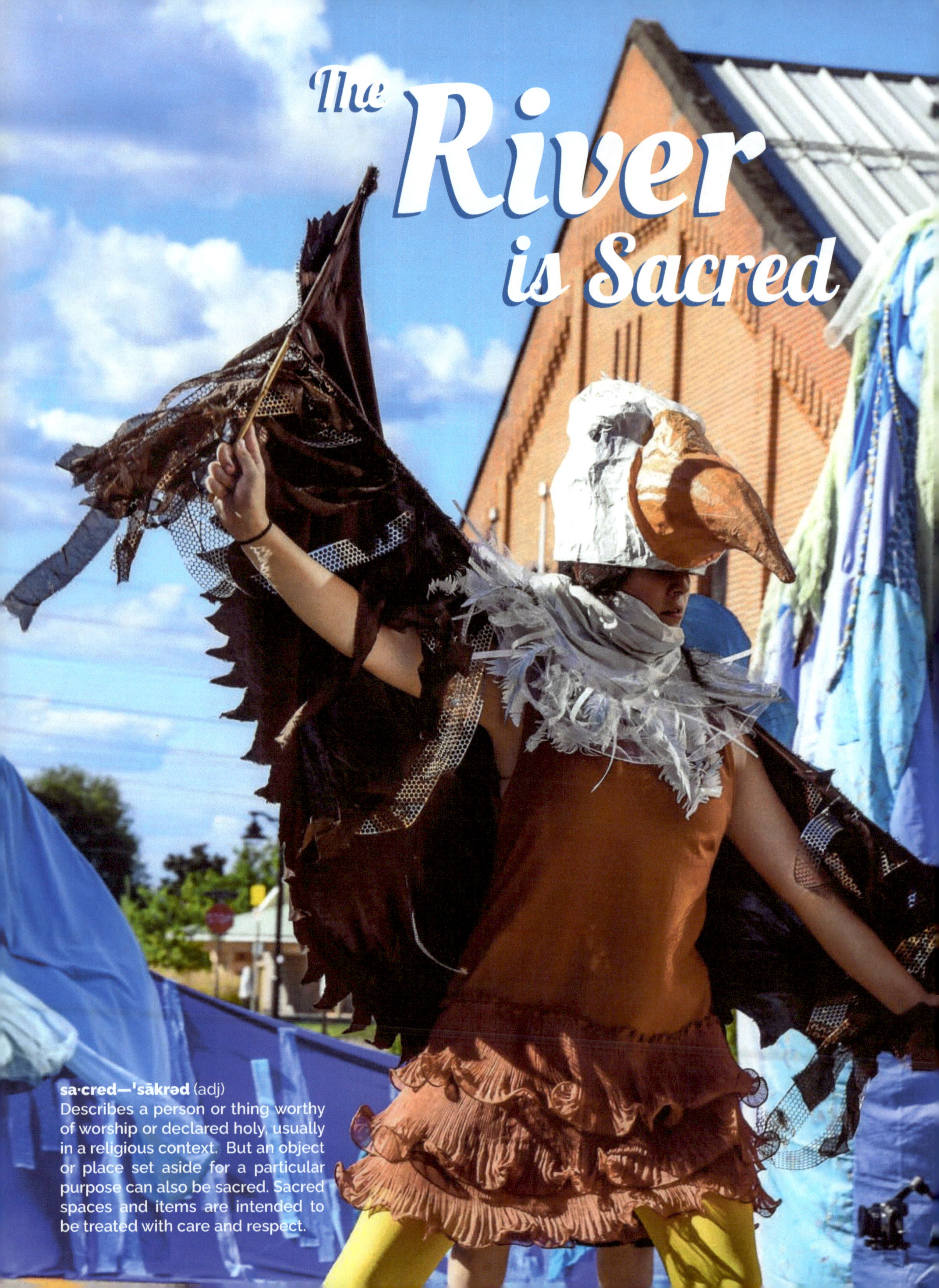

The River is Sacred

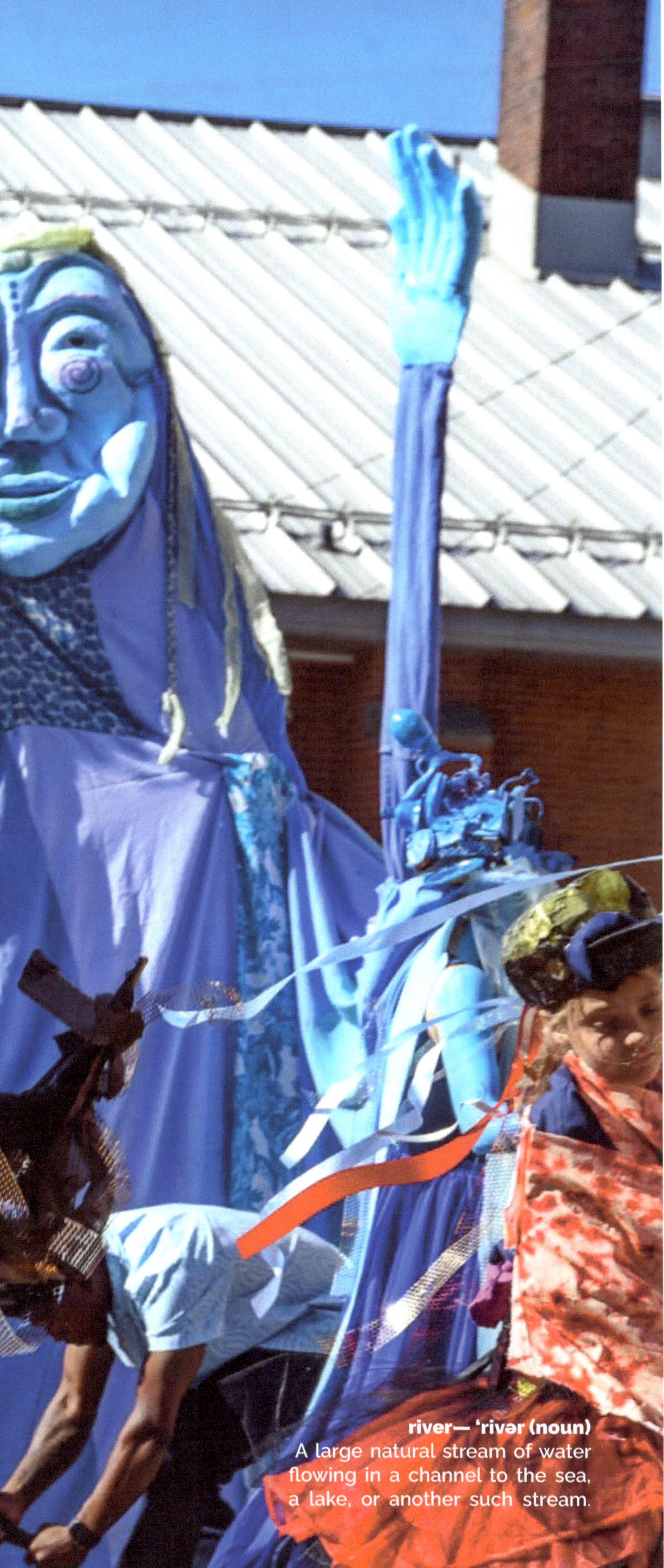

The River is Sacred....

As part of a community arts collective at Studio Dreamshare, I dabble in many media, mostly collaboratively. During the pandemic, making art together was hard, and sometimes forbidden. This presented a creative challenge. *New Patterns in the Kitchesippi Watershed*, the short film, was born from that challenge. The film follows Red Spirits, characters made of recycled objects and red silk, together but spaced apart, creating a giant pattern in the snowy landscape with snowshoes, with thanks for support from Ottawa Valley Community Arts and the Ontario Trillium Foundation. (Search it by name on YouTube to view the film.)

The River is Sacred began as an iteration of that project—Blue Spirits patterned after the Red Spirits—with an ecological theme. I was working on a film in Toronto this winter with Ruth Howard and Jumblies Theatre, and met an incredible community arts facilitator named Catherine Moeller. We hit it off instantly and I invited her to come to the Ottawa Valley to collaborate on a theatrical performance project with giant puppets. We selected a diverse group of soulful artists of all ages—young-at-hearts—to gather for an intense week of co-creation. In true community arts style, our visions about *The River is Sacred*, Catherine's puppetry genius, and the wonderful contributions of each and every group member made this project come to life in the unique and playful way it did.

This project was made possible with the support of EcoPembroke, Calvin and Wesley United Churches, and in particular, Reverend Tiina Cote, whose deep commitment to environmental justice flows through *The River is Sacred*.

Cameron Dreamshare, *Creative Director at Studio Dreamshare*

23

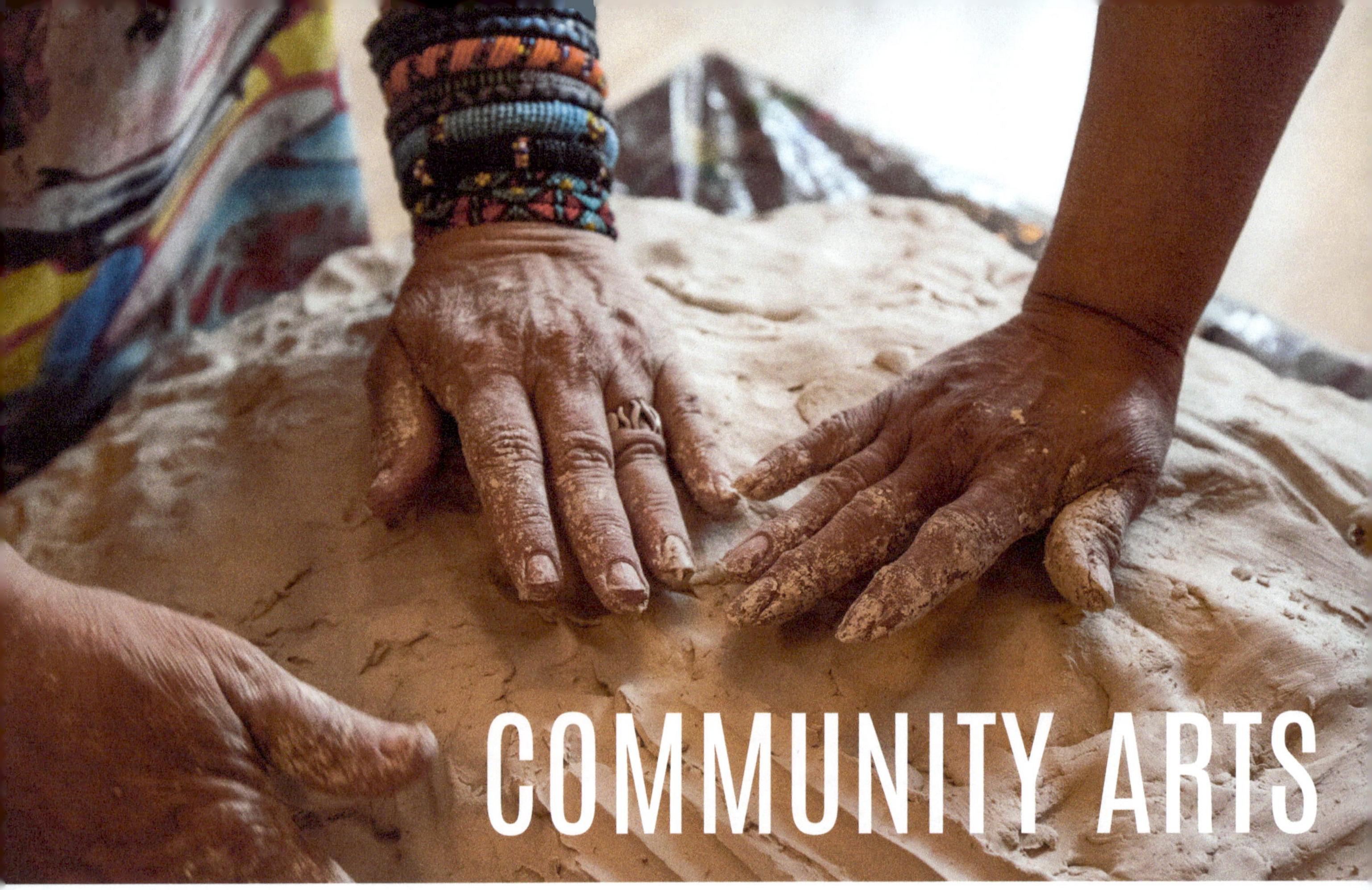

COMMUNITY ARTS

A short history of giant puppets

Catherine Moeller, community artist from Toronto of Clay and Paper Theatre, provided historical context of giant puppets to the Pembroke puppet-making team, whose efforts were on display for the community at CultureFest 2022. Read on for a synopsis of her presentation!

Puppets are an ancient form of art, and giant puppets have a long history throughout the world.

Called gigantes in Europe, the use of giant puppets is widespread across that continent, some of which make annual appearances like Gog and Magog, guardians of the city of London who have been paraded through the city streets since the time of King Henry V.

In the north of France, the tradition of the "gayants" dates back to 1480 where large figures are carried through the city each July. Today, the main figure is over eight metres tall, weighs over 300 kilos and requires eight bearers.

The Dutch people first introduced giant, grotesque figures in 1771 during a procession commemorating the French defeat when attempting to recapture one of their towns. Various Christian celebrations in Spain and Portugal utilize giant figures to symbolize evil spirits conquered by Christ which are burned in bonfires, or fallas, at the end of the festivals.

Presently, giant puppets appear in Brazil's carnival, Dublin's St. Patrick's Day Parade, the festival of Dussehra in India, China's New Year parades, and throughout Africa where many tribes make effigies of dead people as part of the funeral ceremony.

Bread and Puppet Theater began in New York and moved to Vermont, and is one of the most influential and inspirational puppetry groups of the 20th century. In addition to entertainment, Bread and Puppet Theater is a politically radical theatre that drew attention to many social issues in the community, and broadened out to larger street protests about the Vietnam War.

Clay and Paper Theatre was founded in 1994 by David Anderson, theatre activist, producer of new Canadian work, and defender of public space. From his earliest days David's fervent wish was to eliminate barriers to experiencing theatre and tell contemporary stories using ancient techniques in bold and arresting ways.

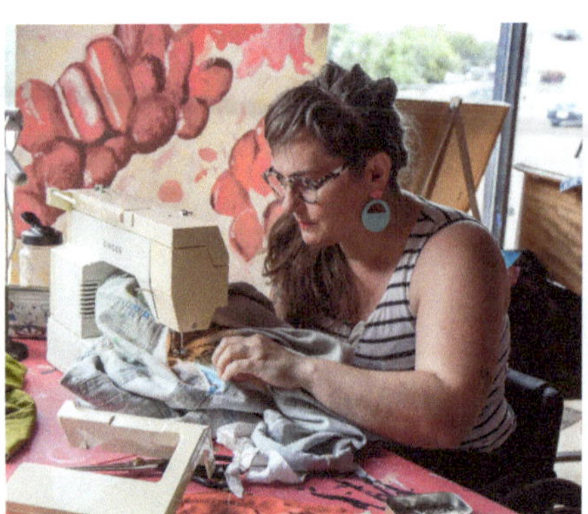
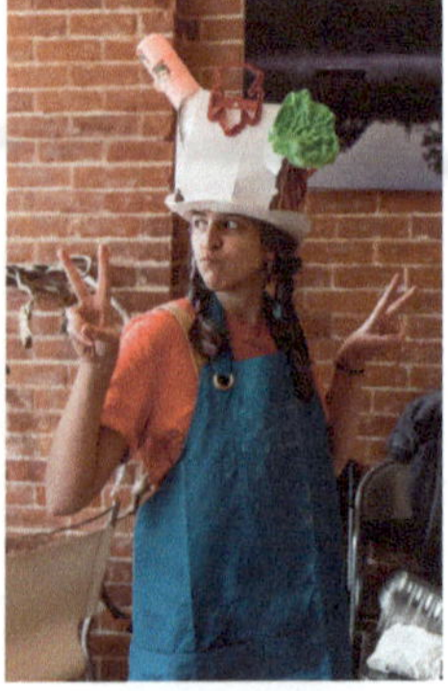

"Community Arts saved my life during the pandemic, by giving me a community."—Rose

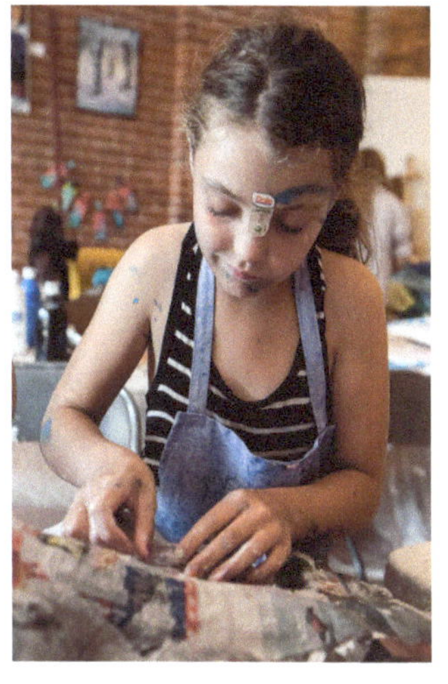

In 2014 Tamara Romanchuk became co-artistic director and continues to champion and grow David's vision of a "theatre without walls". The theatre's work is still inspired by oral traditions, folk tales, songs, poems, and fables, local stories, history, and current social issues, embracing an aesthetic that honours ancient traditions in performance (commedia dell'arte, puppetry, mask, pageantry, spectacle, street theatre) and tools (clay and paper), and then reinvents them for today's urgent storytelling needs.

Studio Dreamshare tapped into Catherine's expertise to create a 5-metre tall puppet representing the Sacred River, a genderless wise grandparent figure requiring two or three performers to bring to life. In one week, the energetic group created nine papier maché heads with full costumes representing birds and river animals, including a three-metre-long eel that eats one of the polluting people right out of their boat. What is most remarkable is that 16 people ranging in age from nine to almost 70 created from scratch and mostly from recycled materials, the full ensemble and a 17-minute show that highlighted environmental issues affecting our sacred rivers.

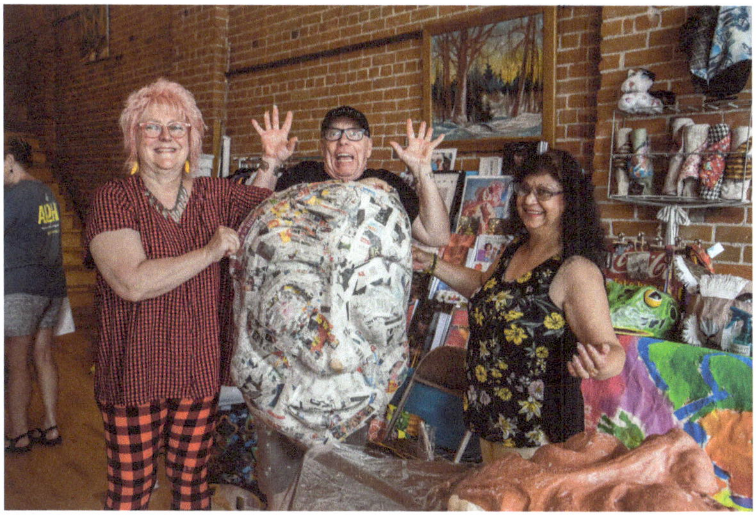

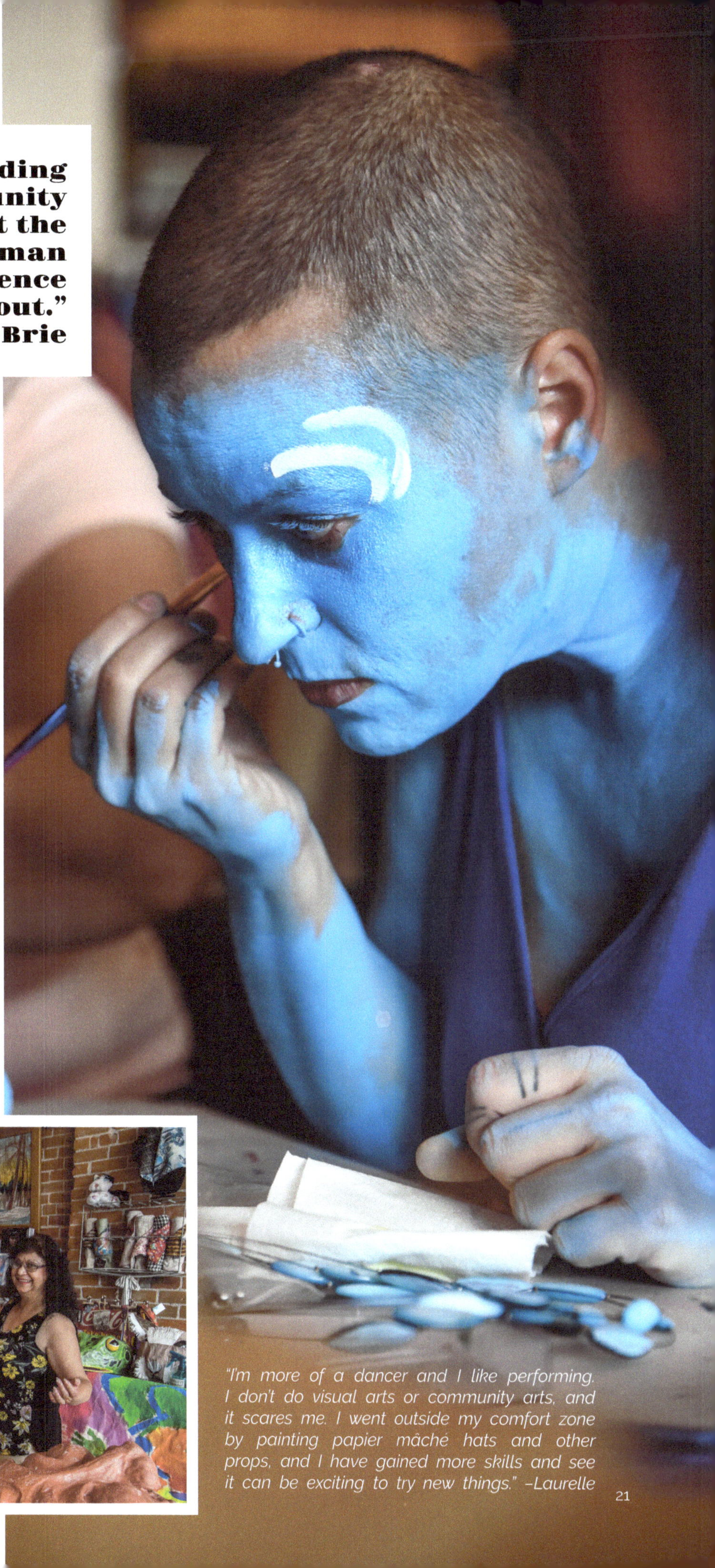

Community Art—An Intergenerational Experience

Studio Dreamshare is a valuable asset in our community promoting intergenerational team spirit. The giant puppet workshop was attended by youth as young as nine years of age to seniors. My experience with intergenerational socializing and working together towards a common goal was not only stimulating and rewarding but important for raising awareness, learning and mentoring, building a community and breaking down barriers.

Today's families are geographically widespread. Families do not always have access to grandchildren, grandparents, aunts, uncles and cousins. In my experience this community arts project provided a great family experience where adults and children could interact, socialize, mentor, learn and teach. As our youngest members commented, "I like working with adults, especially when they are super artistic. I'm learning a lot from them."

In this digital age, youth build skills in problem solving and technology, however, creative skills, arts and imagination are sometimes compromised. Intergenerational projects allow an exchange of skills and promote team work in a world that tends toward technological isolation. Learning is reciprocal: youth learn from the ways and life experiences of the elders and elders learn technological and other skills from youth. Furthermore, the exchange in communication provides insights into the world of today's youth and their challenges. These conversations between the generations bring out perspectives which help close the generational gap and improve mutual understanding.

Community arts projects are centred on raising awareness and building community spirit. This project was related to environmental issues, which greatly affects the youth of today. It is important to actively engage youth in such projects to foster global thinking and encourage actions to improve their local community.

I was surprised at, and so impressed with the young participants. We had one particularly brilliant youth who was very interesting to talk to, and our youngest member was a real self-starter, very motivated, took charge and got things done. On the whole, adults and youth alike demonstrated great interest, knowledge, willingness to assist, problem solve, learn with enthusiasm and interacted with all ages with ease.

Studio Dreamshare provides opportunities for intergenerational projects, common goals, to share creative ideas, troubleshoot and resolve problems, creating a community that is inclusive and respectful of everyone, regardless of age, gender and race.

Suli Adams is a retired scientist who volunteers for many local community organizations, a staff writer for an international dancer's magazine, and a member of the International Dance Council CID, UNESCO (The United Nations of Dance).

"I am always open to challenges and learning new things; it makes us grow."—Suli

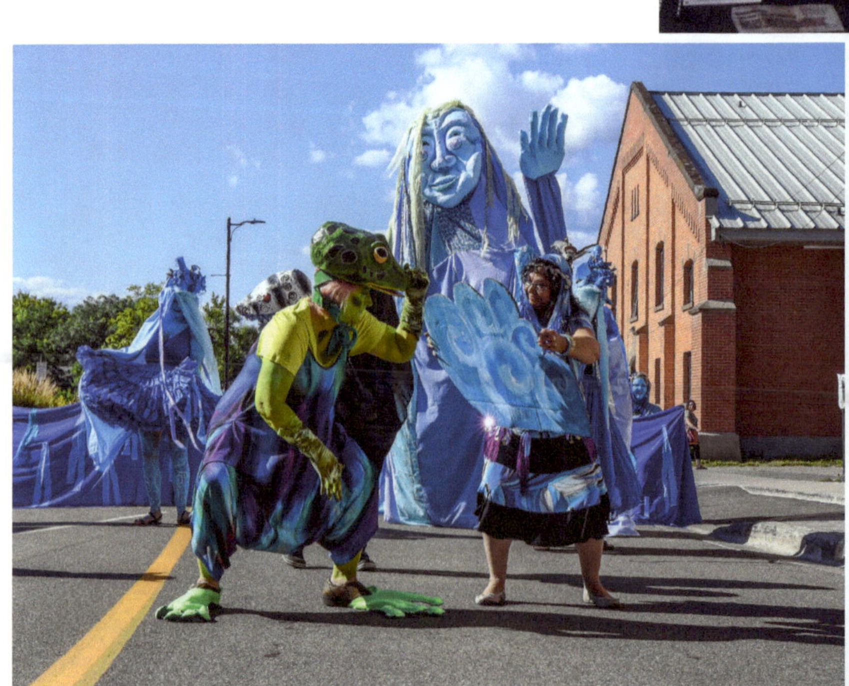

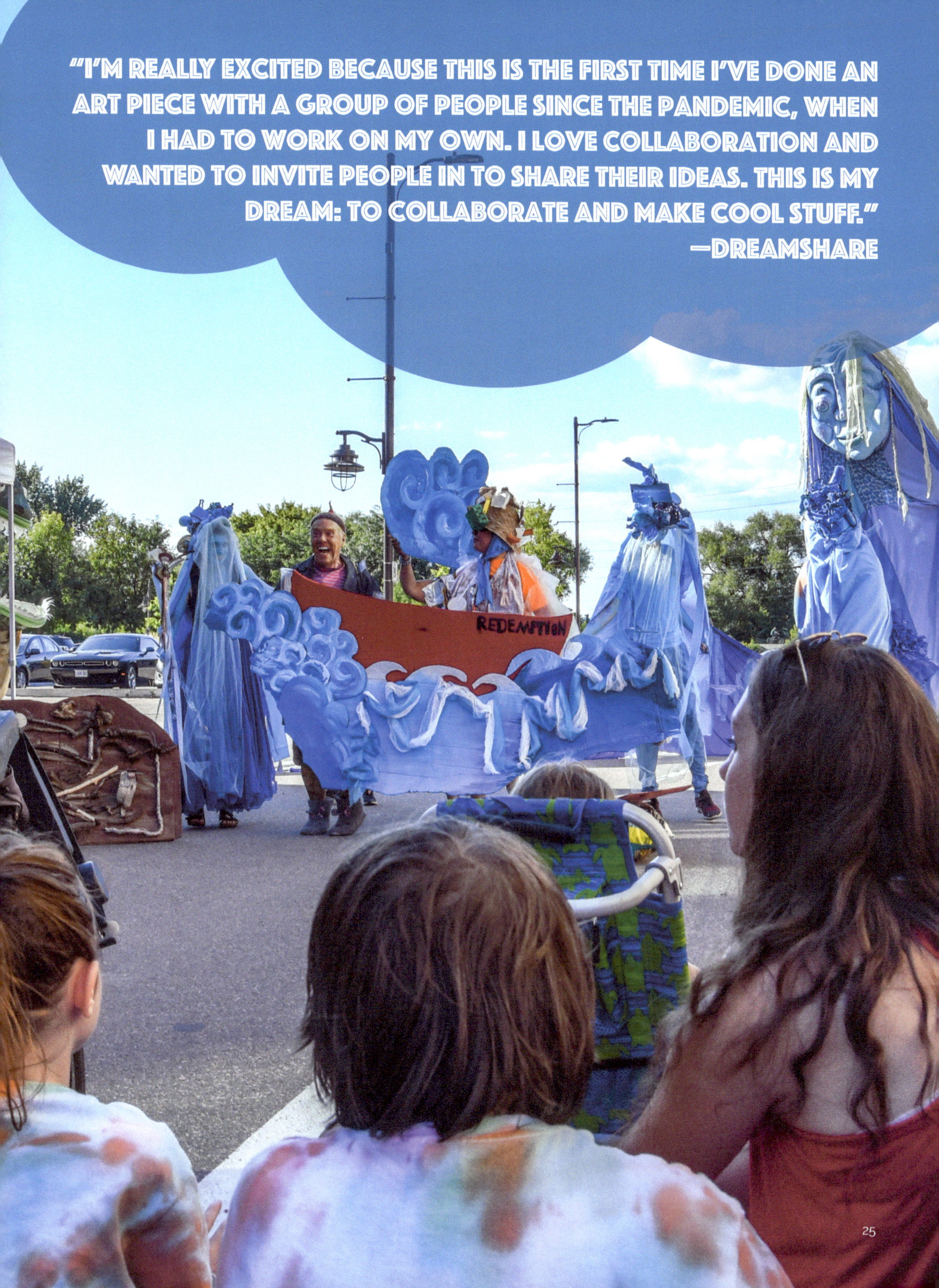

"I'M REALLY EXCITED BECAUSE THIS IS THE FIRST TIME I'VE DONE AN ART PIECE WITH A GROUP OF PEOPLE SINCE THE PANDEMIC, WHEN I HAD TO WORK ON MY OWN. I LOVE COLLABORATION AND WANTED TO INVITE PEOPLE IN TO SHARE THEIR IDEAS. THIS IS MY DREAM: TO COLLABORATE AND MAKE COOL STUFF."
—DREAMSHARE

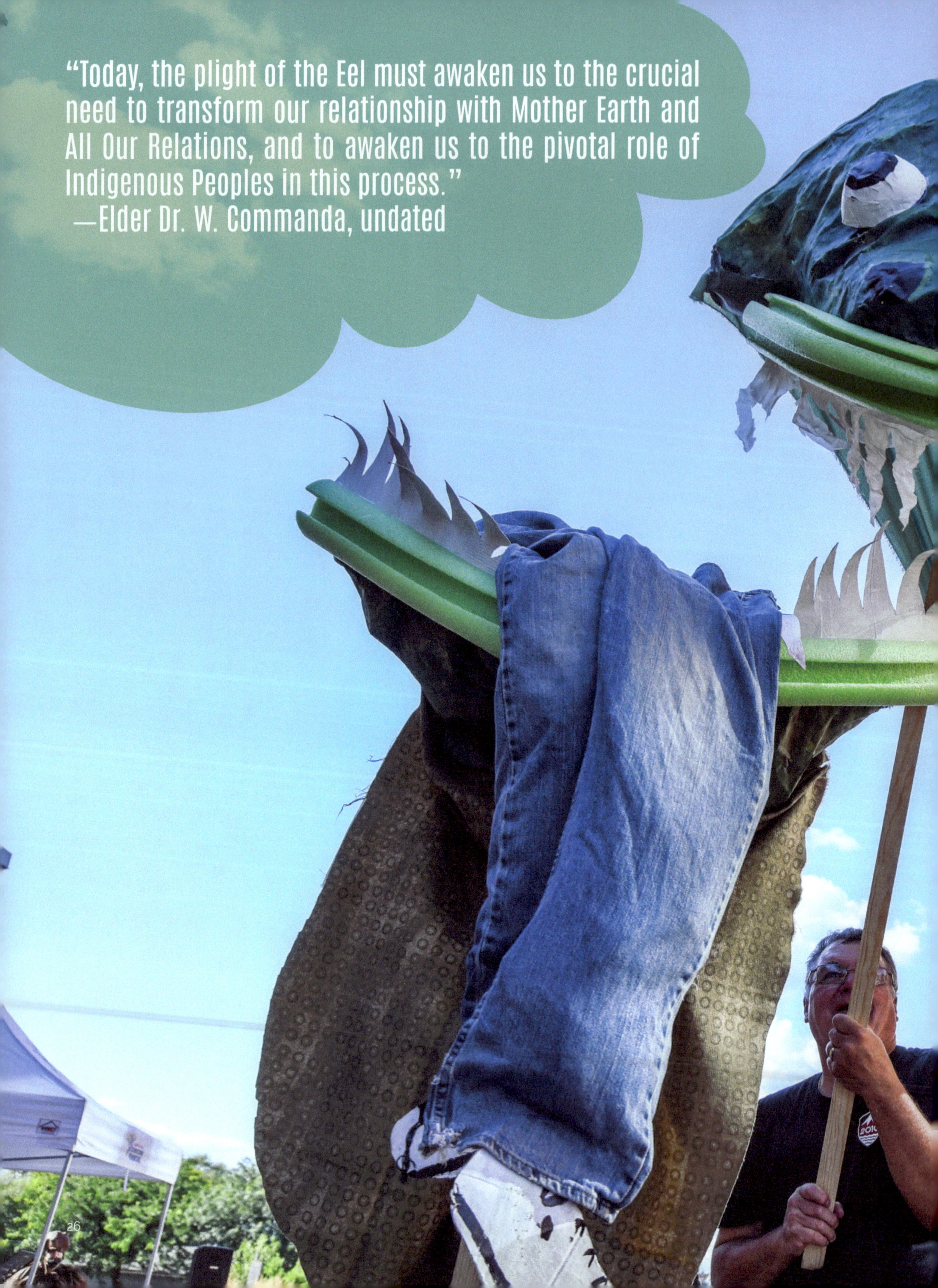
"Today, the plight of the Eel must awaken us to the crucial need to transform our relationship with Mother Earth and All Our Relations, and to awaken us to the pivotal role of Indigenous Peoples in this process."
—Elder Dr. W. Commanda, undated

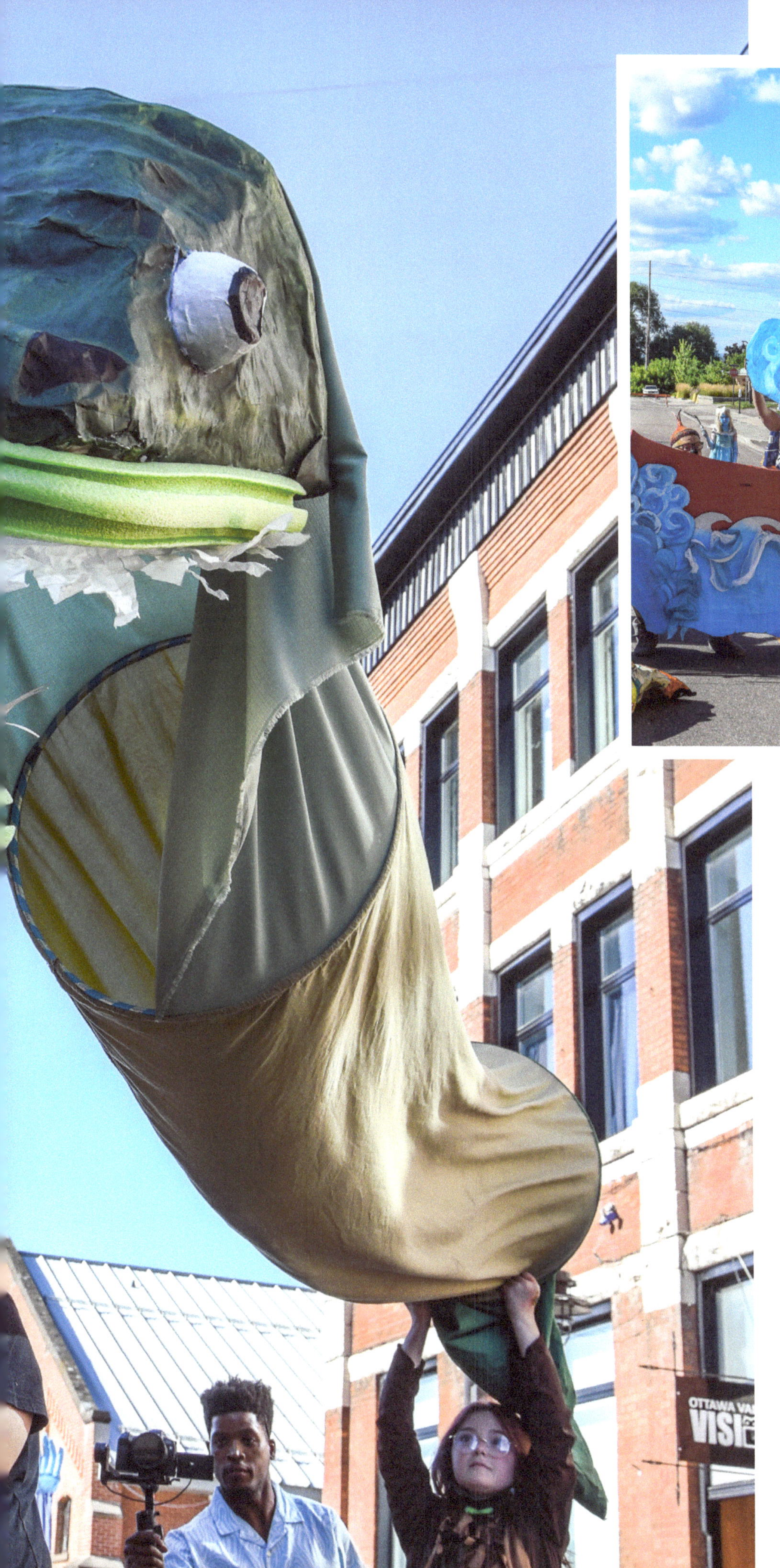

Kichesippi (Kichi Sibi, Kitcisipi)

This is the Algonquin term for the Ottawa River that translates to 'big river,' a 1200 km waterway that extends from Montréal to Lake Temiskaming. The Kichesippi was a critical highway for the Algonquin and Métis, facilitating life, trade and delivery of fur and timber.

Kichisippi Pimisi

The Indigenous name for the American Eel, sacred to the Algonquin people and their culture as a provider of nourishment, medicine and spiritual inspiration. It was once abundant throughout Algonquin Traditional Territory and has suffered dramatic population decline. Kichisippi Pimisi is a central figure in *The River is Sacred*, appearing in large puppet form, and providing a lesson to all about caring for our world.

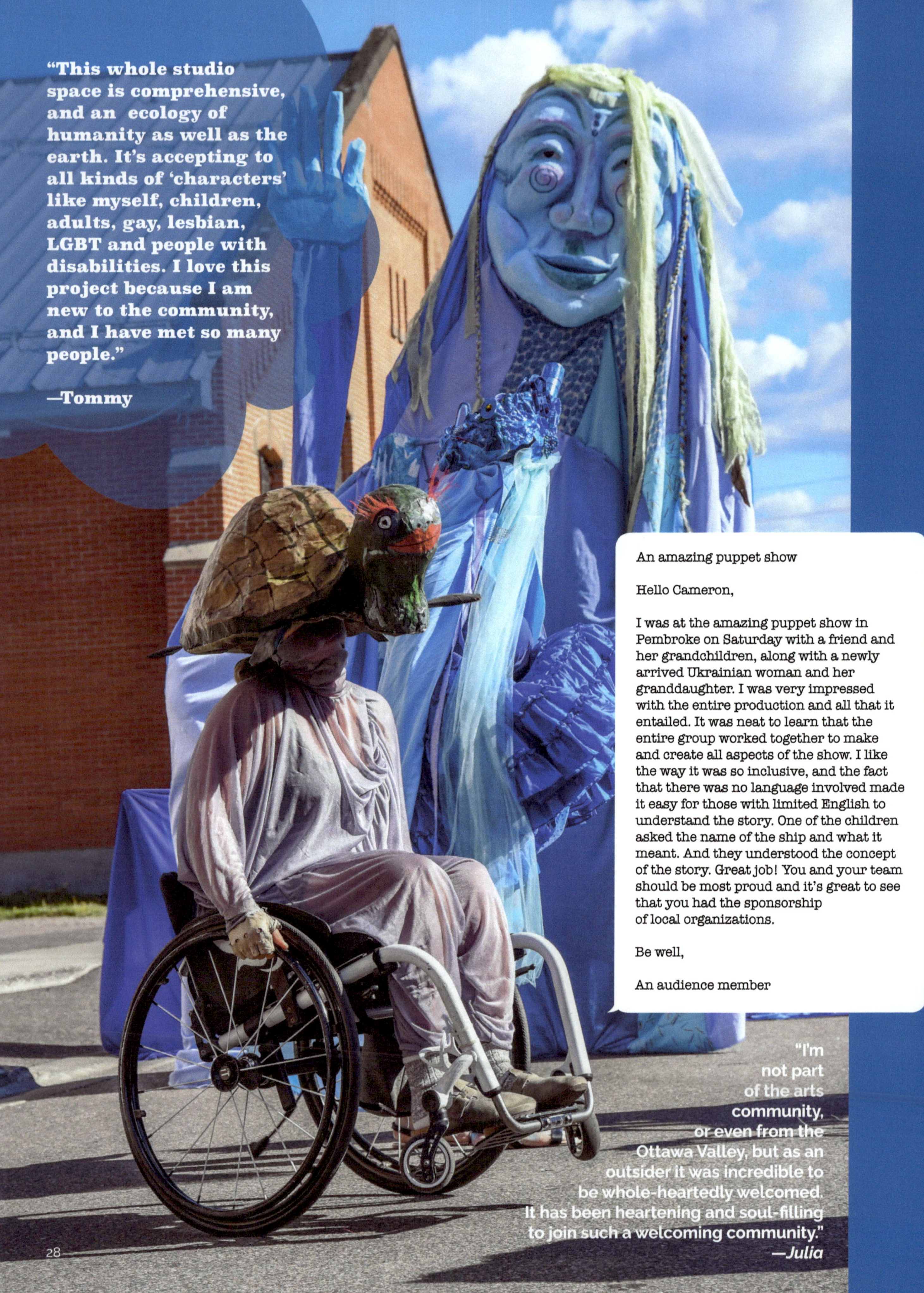

"This whole studio space is comprehensive, and an ecology of humanity as well as the earth. It's accepting to all kinds of 'characters' like myself, children, adults, gay, lesbian, LGBT and people with disabilities. I love this project because I am new to the community, and I have met so many people."

—Tommy

An amazing puppet show

Hello Cameron,

I was at the amazing puppet show in Pembroke on Saturday with a friend and her grandchildren, along with a newly arrived Ukrainian woman and her granddaughter. I was very impressed with the entire production and all that it entailed. It was neat to learn that the entire group worked together to make and create all aspects of the show. I like the way it was so inclusive, and the fact that there was no language involved made it easy for those with limited English to understand the story. One of the children asked the name of the ship and what it meant. And they understood the concept of the story. Great job! You and your team should be most proud and it's great to see that you had the sponsorship of local organizations.

Be well,

An audience member

"I'm not part of the arts community, or even from the Ottawa Valley, but as an outsider it was incredible to be whole-heartedly welcomed. It has been heartening and soul-filling to join such a welcoming community."
—Julia

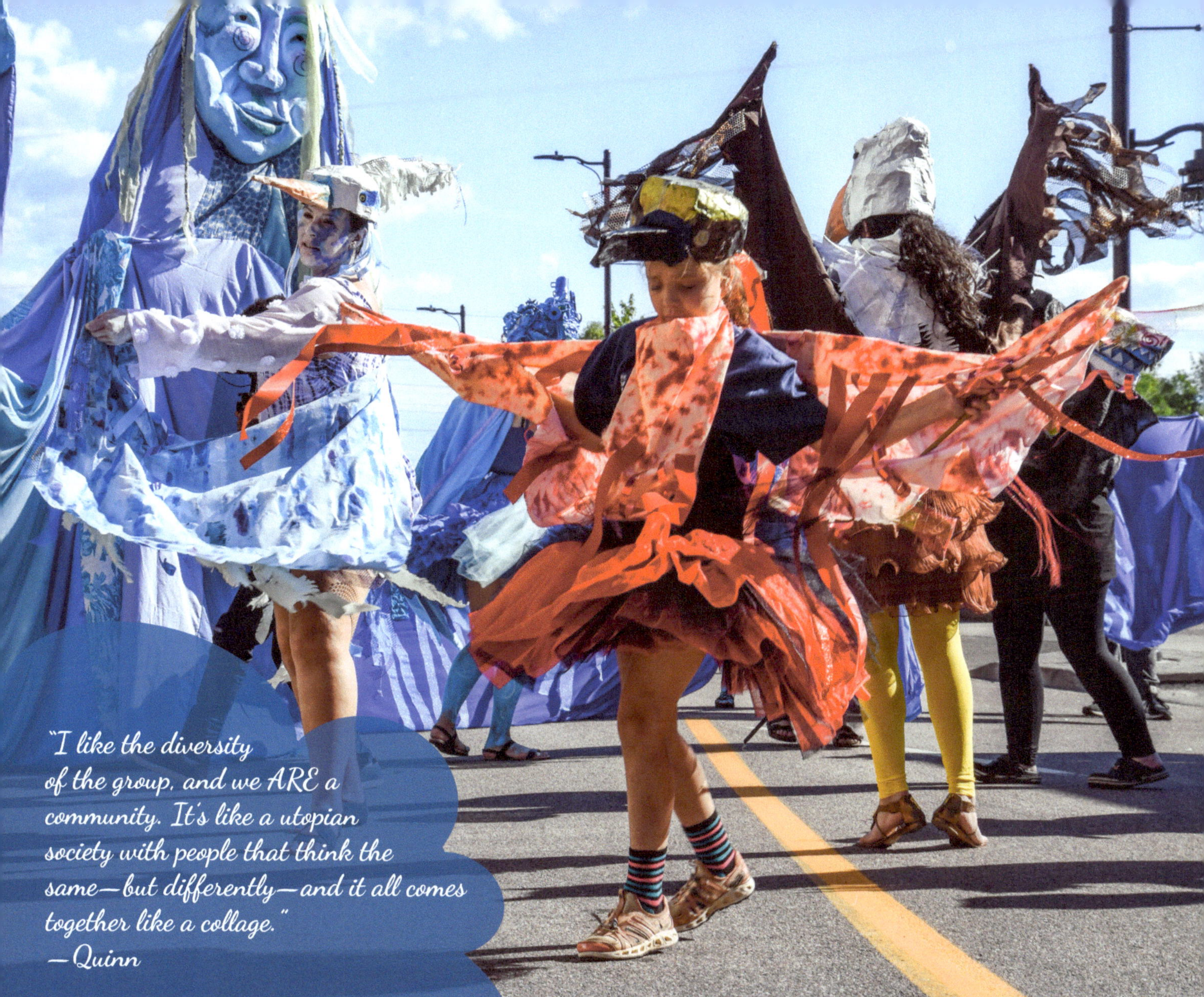

"Last year in Rainbow Art Club we went to the marina and helped pick up cigarette butts and garbage on land. Others pulled garbage out of the water, and the things they pulled out! Four shopping carts, parts from a car, two bikes, a scooter and other stuff. It was all laid out on the grass and we just went around and looked at it. I filled a 19 litre (5 gallon) bucket just with cigarette butts, and we all collected a bucket of garbage each. It was frustrating to see so much garbage. The week after we cleaned, I went back to the marina, and there were cigarette butts everywhere. I see them everywhere now, and there is a lot of garbage laying around. I just feel there needs to be another solution."
—Alex/Nox

"Dreamshare assembled a motley crew of people of different ages, genders, sexual orientations, ethnicities, physical abilities and from different places to create a community. An unsuspecting group, because no one really knew what we were going to accomplish (including Dreamshare), we all trusted in Dreamshare and the process of making meaningful art. Respect emanated from each and every group member, and our community was built with each layer of papier mâché, of which there were many. Many layers to our community and to our papier mâché."
—Darlene

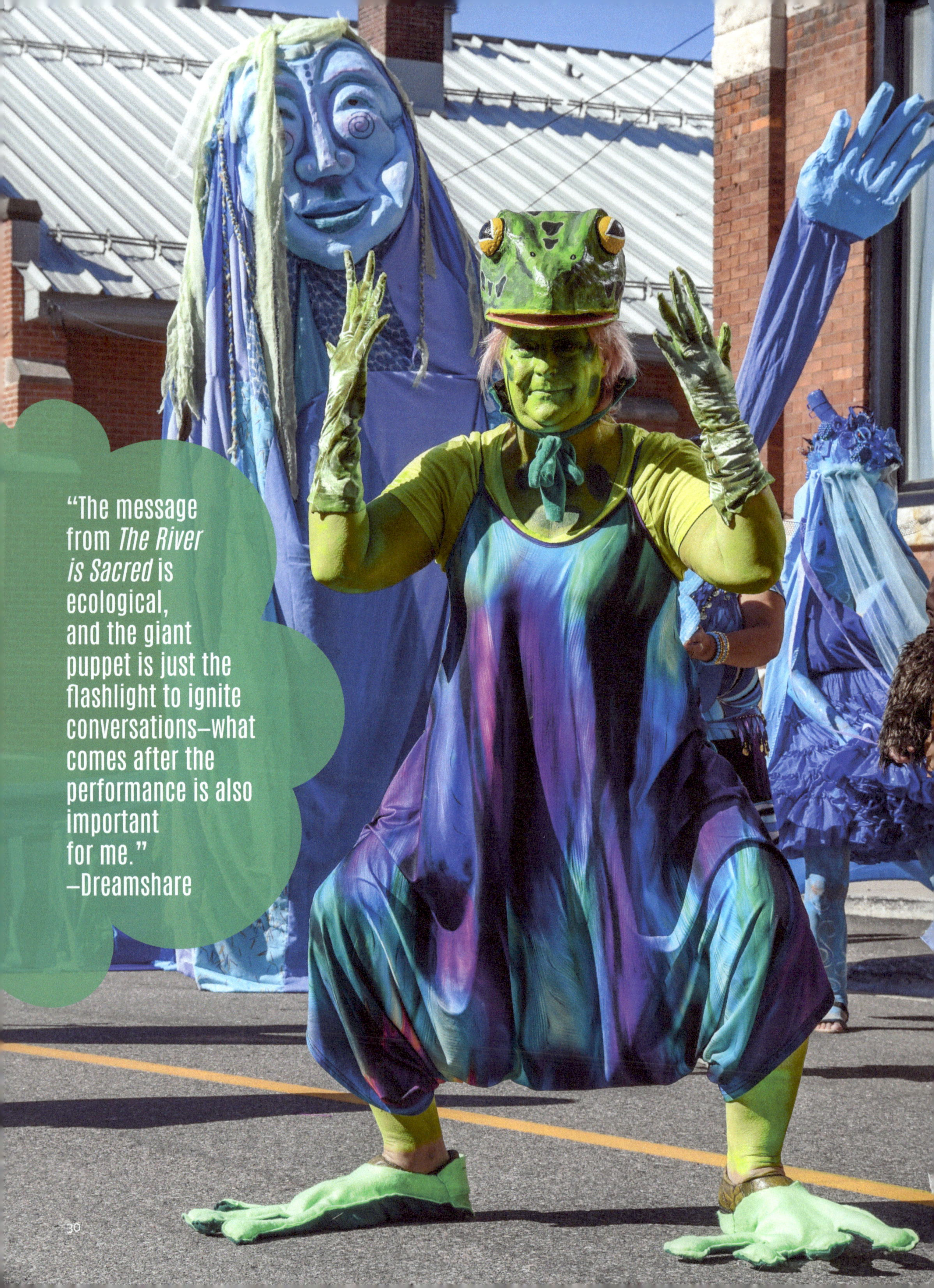

"The message from *The River is Sacred* is ecological, and the giant puppet is just the flashlight to ignite conversations—what comes after the performance is also important for me."
—Dreamshare

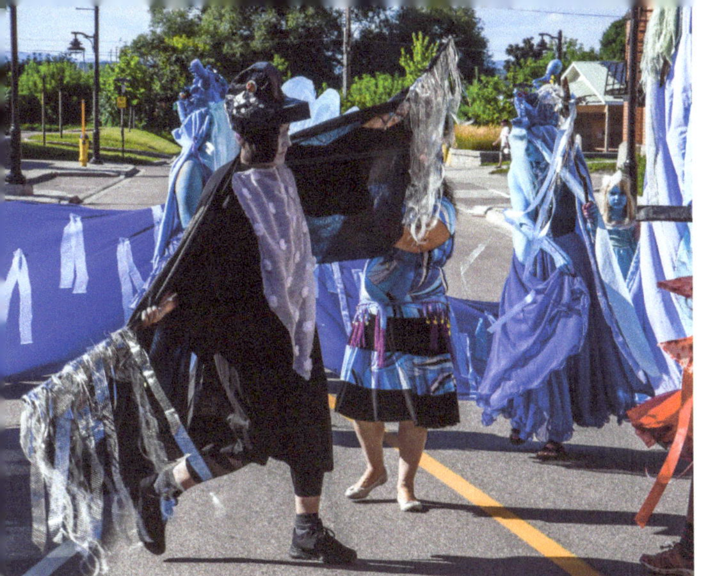

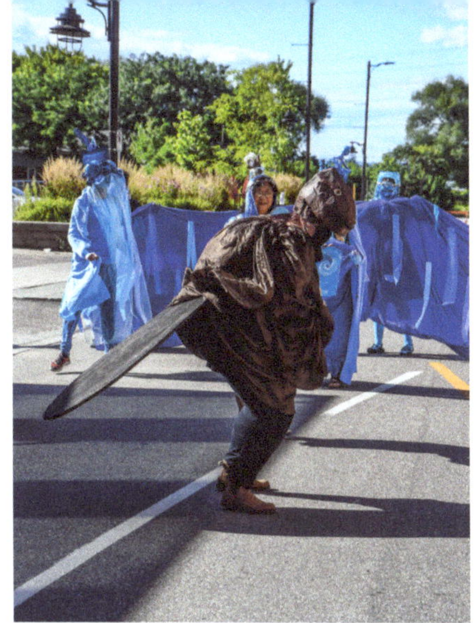

"The performance is a gorgeous display of eco-consciousness brought to life in all these beautiful colours."
—Rose

"Arts are a great way to connect with people on environmental concerns. It's accessible because it isn't literary, academic,or propaganda. The message can be absorbed in an emotional, human way."
—Brie

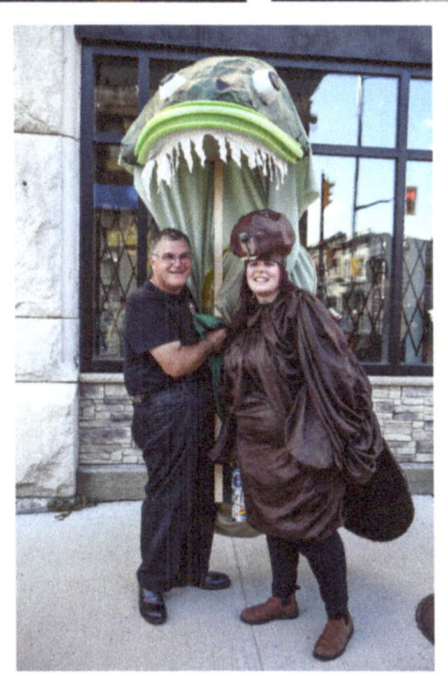

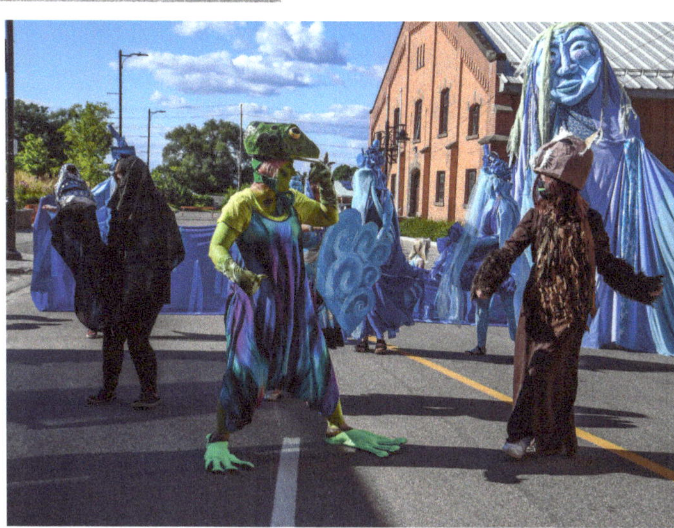

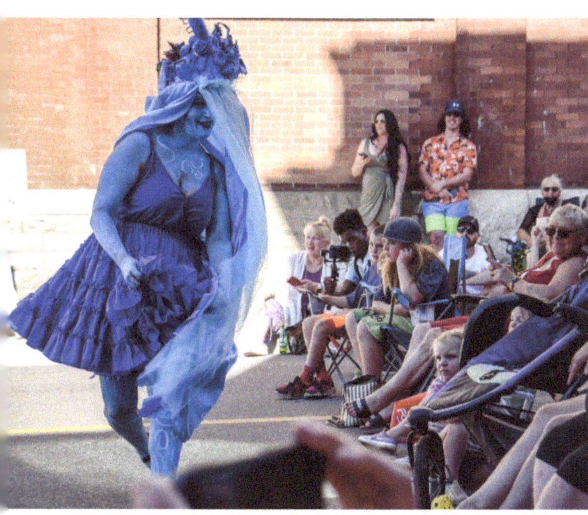

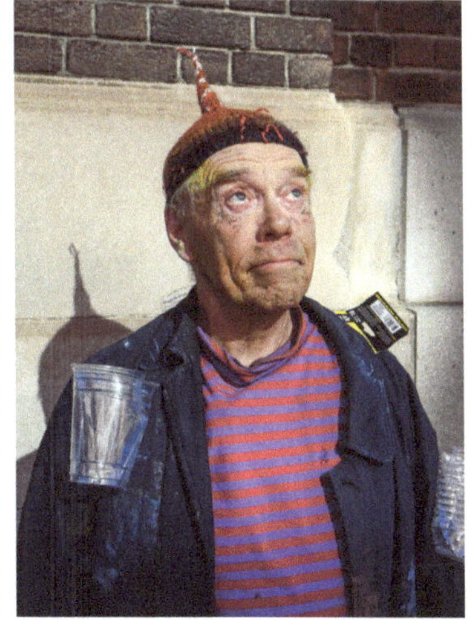

"This has been the coolest thing ever: making giant puppets and small puppets for an actual parade. That's big—literally and figuratively!! It has meant so much to me to be a part of this project so I can practise my art and hopefully be the new Bob Ross."
—Cohen

"I was glad to bring awareness to environmental issues. I don't talk about it anywhere else in my life."
—Clare

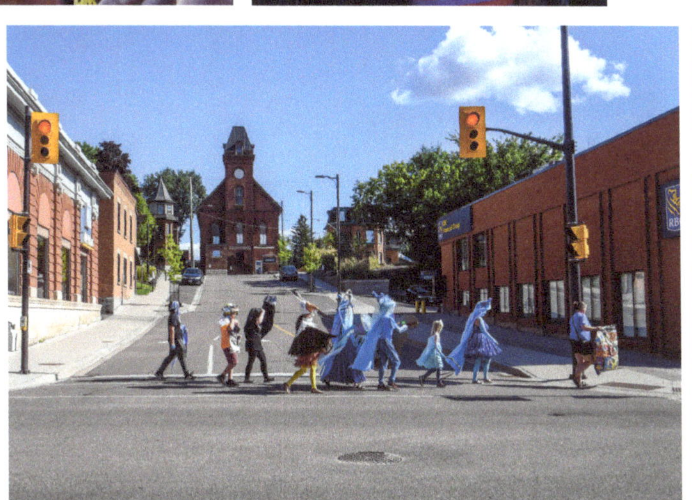

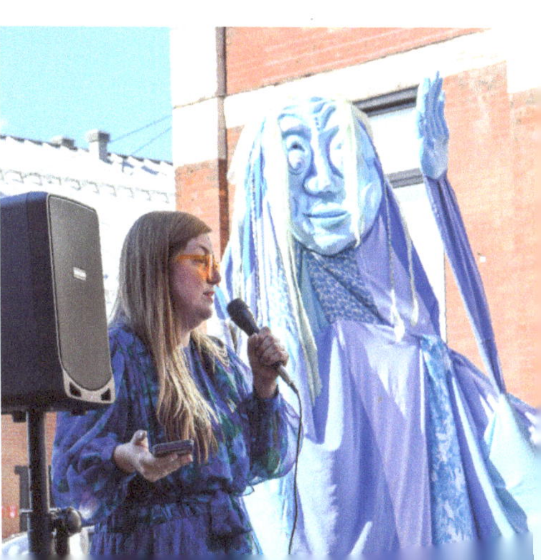

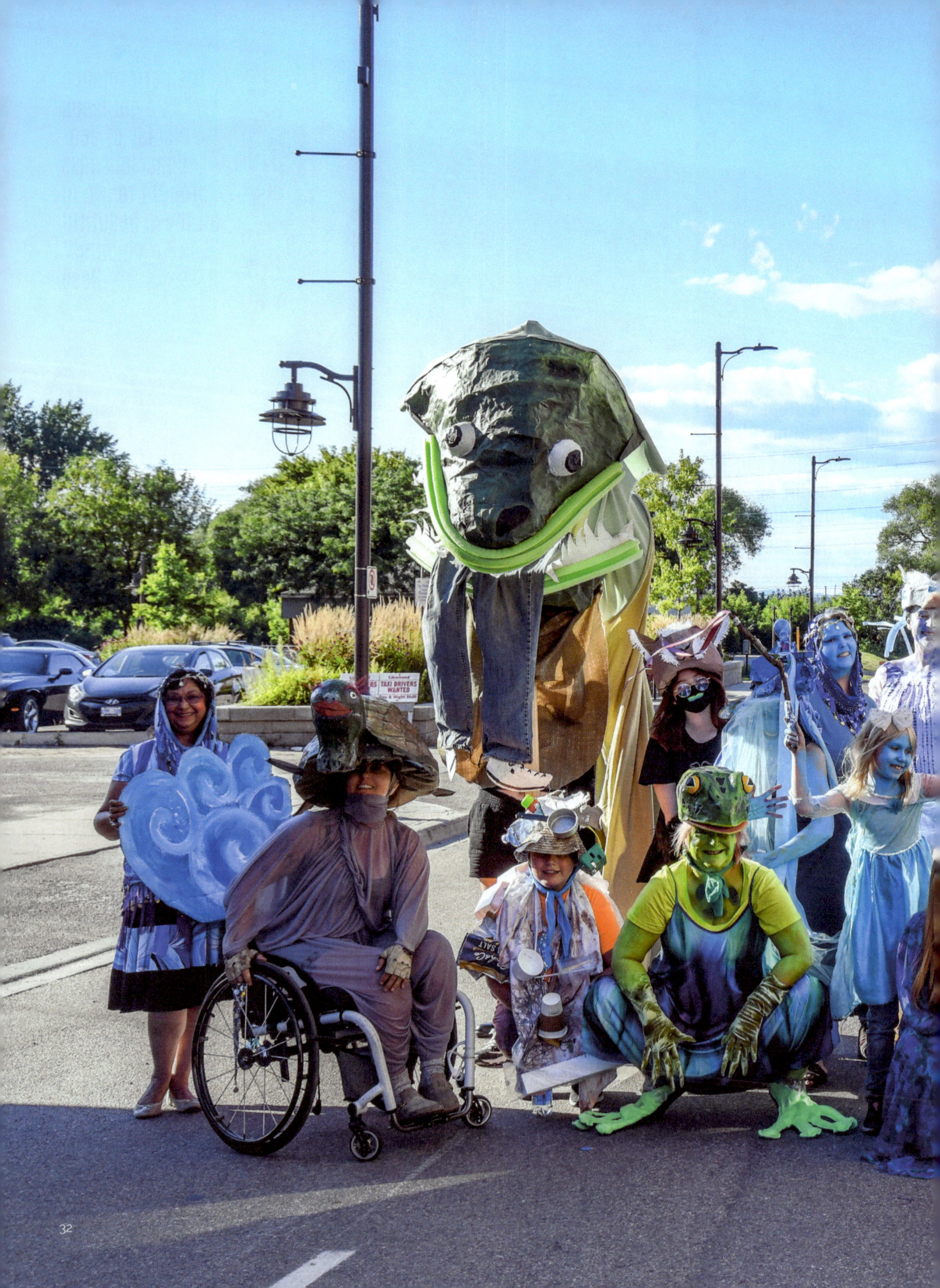

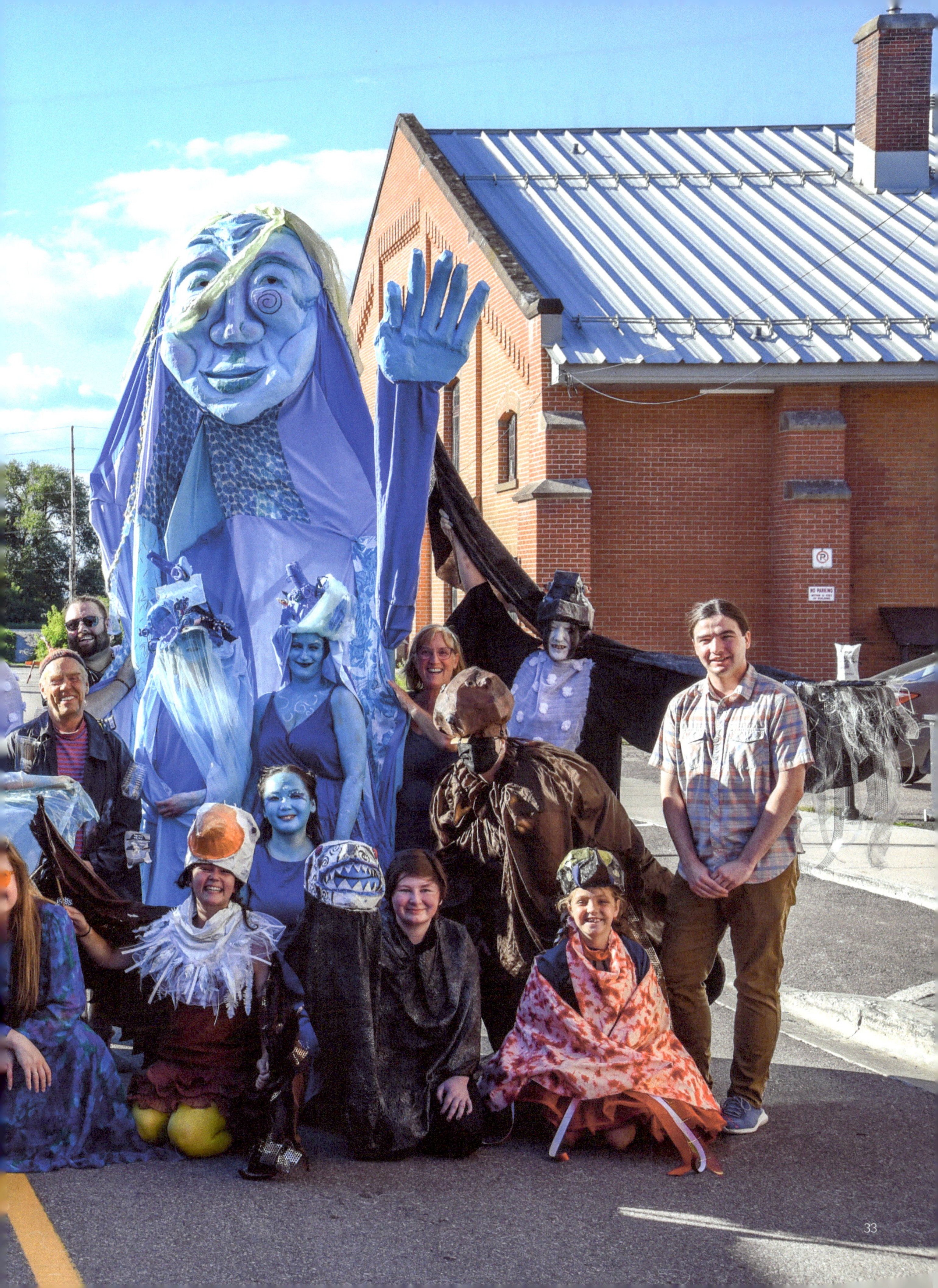

ECO GRIEF

Grief and anxiety are all-encompassing emotional reactions to perceived threats: our head, heart, and body are all activated during these experiences of worry and mourning. I often catch myself describing what "makes me so sad" or "gives me anxiety", as though these are outside forces that I've suddenly encountered. Actually, all of our emotions—even the challenging ones like grief and anxiety—come from us. Intense emotions serve the purpose of keeping us safe; they show up with gut-level, deep evolutionary responses that allow us to adapt and survive amidst chaos. In this way, we understand that our panic and mourning are natural, understandable, and fully human reactions to the ongoing climate crisis.

The history of Earth is full of extinctions and climate crises, but as far as we know, this era that we call the Anthropocene is the first time that the combined actions of a single species (humans) has shifted the global climate. More accurately, current climate change is being caused by the specific actions of a relatively small proportion of all humans living in white-supremacist, capitalist, colonial, ableist, heteropatriarchal, cis-normative societies that disproportionately impacts everyone else. This definitely brings up grief and anxiety for me...what about you?

Along with my anxiety, I feel focused and passionate because we know that we will be the cause of our extinction unless we choose differently. Human consciousness and human choices are driving climate change right now. Human consciousness and human choices are also malleable, changeable, and resilient. We can do better. We can change.

I know that it sounds like I've been cheerleading for emotional distress so far and it's not my intention to dismiss the really scary sensations that are part of moving through grief and anxiety about our changing climate. When these feelings occur frequently and intensely, they are absolutely more harmful than helpful, and we need to find strategies for managing them to function in wellness, safety, and to achieve our justice goals.

Personally and professionally, the best way that I know how to start managing my grief and anxiety over the human-driven climate crisis is to come back to my favourite ways of reminding myself that I'm not alone in this feeling. I am so grateful for my community networks, especially the relationships that I continue to nurture with my queer and trans, Black and Indigenous kin. The more I learn about authenticity, reciprocity, generosity and integrity from showing up in these relationships, the more I see these connections functioning exactly like the mycelium of mushrooms and fungi: spreading their roots and runners underground to very literally hold this place together; giving the soil strength and stability so that we can weather all kinds of storms.

How does the environment reflect our nature back to us? What is possible when we choose—truly and on purpose choose— to be in respectful, reciprocal relationships with First Peoples and Places? What knowledge, experience, wisdom, even solutions to the human-driven climate crisis are available to us when we listen to the messages of our anxiety and grief?

Julianna Morin MSW/RSW,
Psychotherapist

"Eco-grief/climate change anxiety is a big part of my personal journey, and how I am reconnecting, with accountability, to my Indigenous ancestry. It is how I am learning to decentre my white privilege and mobilize the roles and responsibilities that come with the teachings. It speaks to me about what it is to be 7th generation Anishinaabe and to be lighting that 8th fire for the next generations to come."
—Julianna

A series of words spoken from the heart during our talk about eco grief

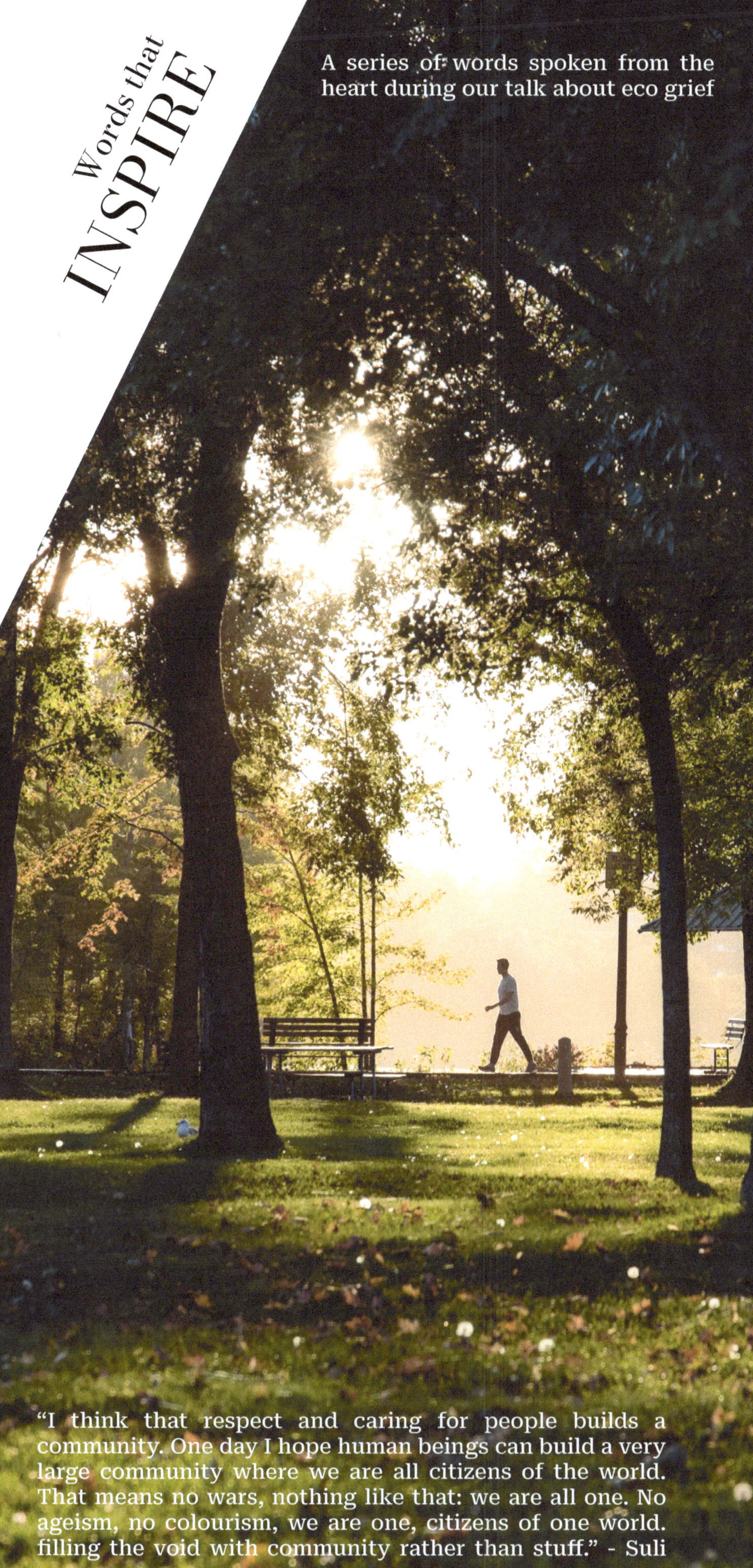

words	ownership
feathers	taking charge
feeling	less
sharing	more
sorrow	do something
meta	now
anxiety	do it, purpose
hopeful	forgive
spark	both and
change	connect
dream	sadness
caring	respect
generations	responsibility
adapting	ownership
ancestry	taking charge
ripples	less
paper	more
heavy	compassion
connection	desire
frustrated	feelings
action	forgiveness
busy	sympathy
contribute	relief
humanity	simple
taking action	tears
voice	sad
strength	mad
louder voice	glad
power	anger
compassion	rock bottom
purpose	animal
activism	broke
join hands	curiosity
build	renewal
life	boundaries
fear	start
respected	end
one step at	openness
a time	seed
shame	grow food
history	work together
rebirth	play
choice	respect
emerging	warming
letting go	rainbows
storytelling	head-space
restorying	priorities
focus	priorities
acceptance	grief
mad	soul
community	respect
community	spirit
planting	resonate
seeds	bread
purpose	prototaxite

"I think that respect and caring for people builds a community. One day I hope human beings can build a very large community where we are all citizens of the world. That means no wars, nothing like that: we are all one. No ageism, no colourism, we are one, citizens of one world. filling the void with community rather than stuff." - Suli

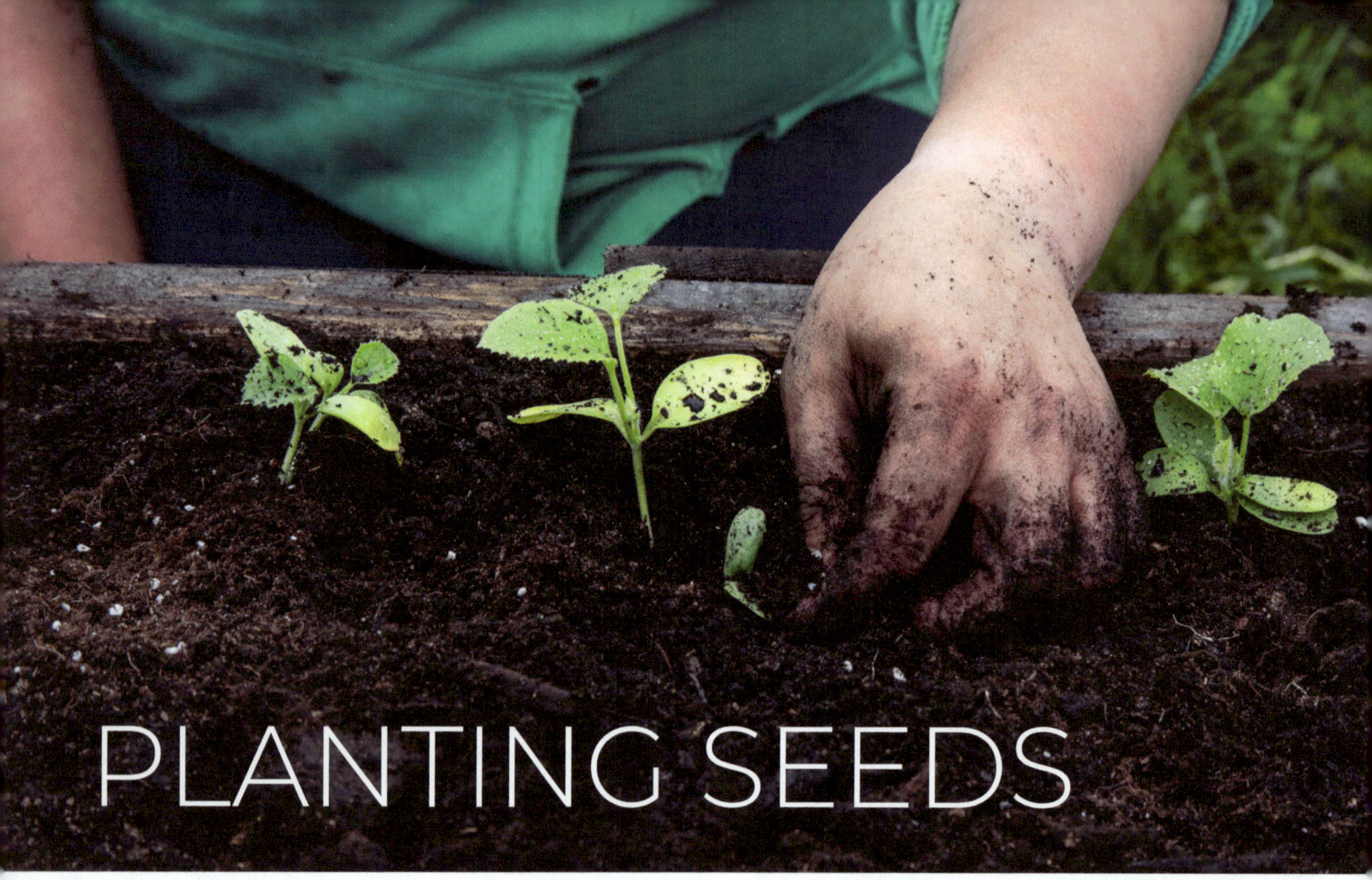

PLANTING SEEDS

Marshall Buchanan (B.Sc.F, M.Sc.F, R.P.F.) co-owner of Ottawa Valley Farm to Fork, is President of the Ottawa Valley Food Co-operative. He is passionate about raising awareness about farming and this past summer dedicated his work to inspiring youth to connect to their local food sources.

In an interview for North Algona Wilberforce Township's newsletter, he commented about why farm work is exciting and meaningful: "Farming is about managing living organisms, such as plants and animals. These all depend on a healthy environment including soils, water, pollinators, microbes and fungi. And then there is the cycle of birth-life-death and renewal, and how this nourishes all the people in the world. Few professions challenge you to think every day about the full cycle of life and our relationship to the earth that sustains us. Or, if you are inventing recipes and selling food to consumers, you can immerse yourself in a whole other frontier of flavour, nutrition, marketing and culture. There's nothing like the reward you get when you know you helped bring a product to market that is nourishing families at their dinner tables."

He elaborates on how many world problems are related to the way we eat or grow our food, and he believes that attracting bright minds to work in the food system will create resiliency, respect, sustainability and culture not just in our food systems, but in our lives.

Alongside the Agri-Food Career Fair, a collaborative project to bring youth to local farms supported by North Algona Wilberforce Township and the Canadian Agricultural Partnership, Marshall hosted a group of youth gardeners and artists from Studio Dreamshare at his farm to learn about the importance of soil health and biodiversity, new and old farming methods, and the joys of connecting more deeply with the land through farming.

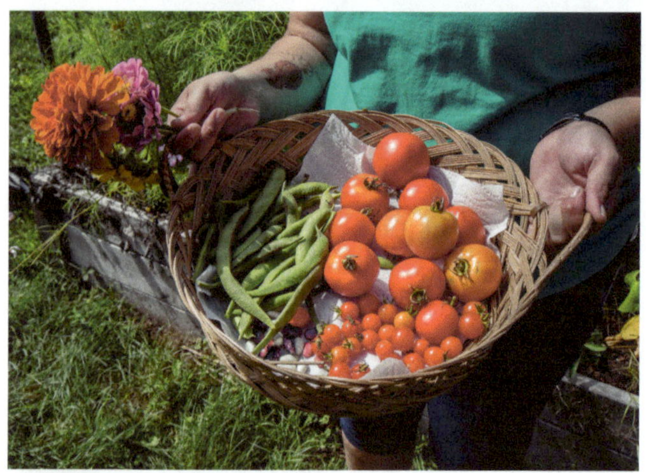

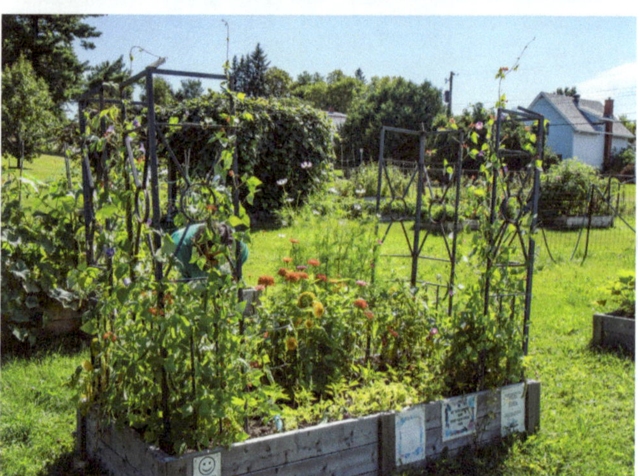

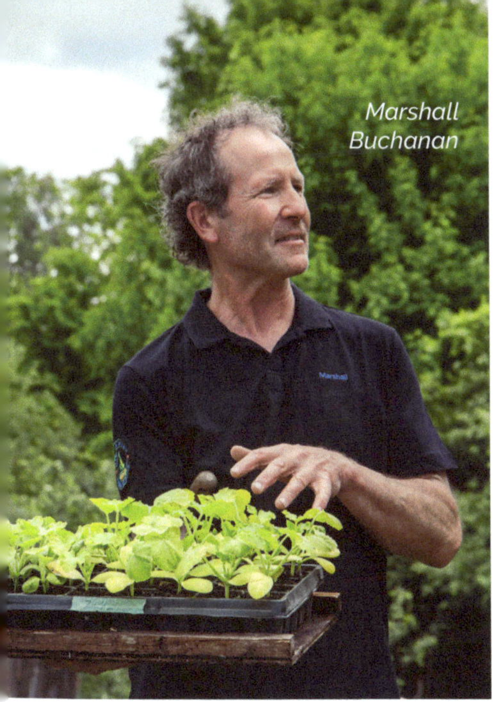

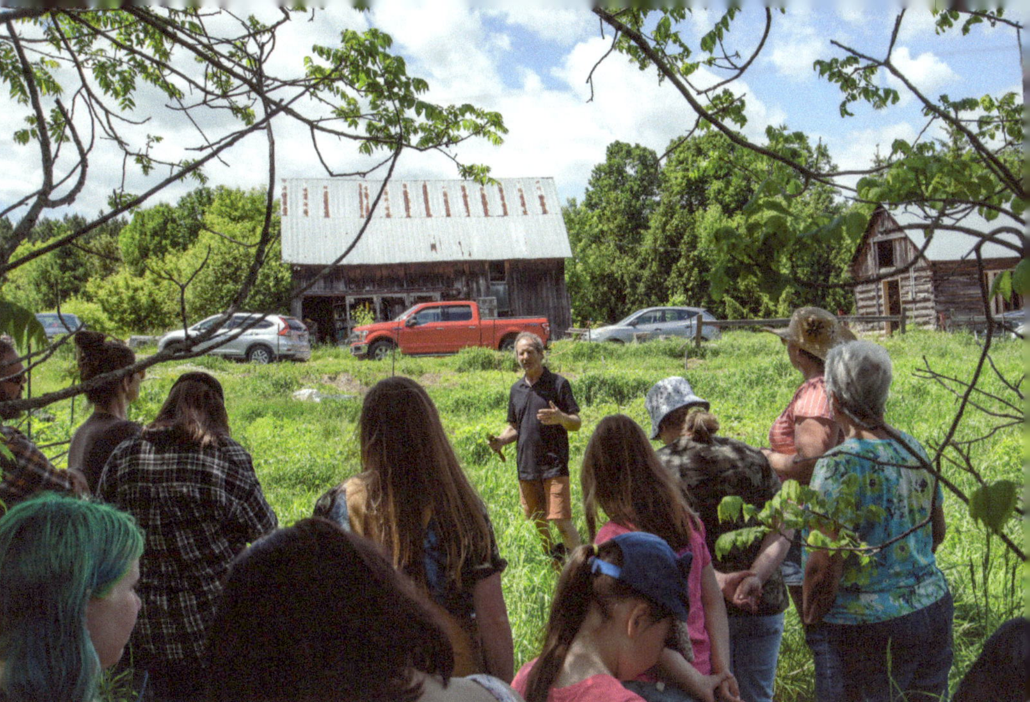

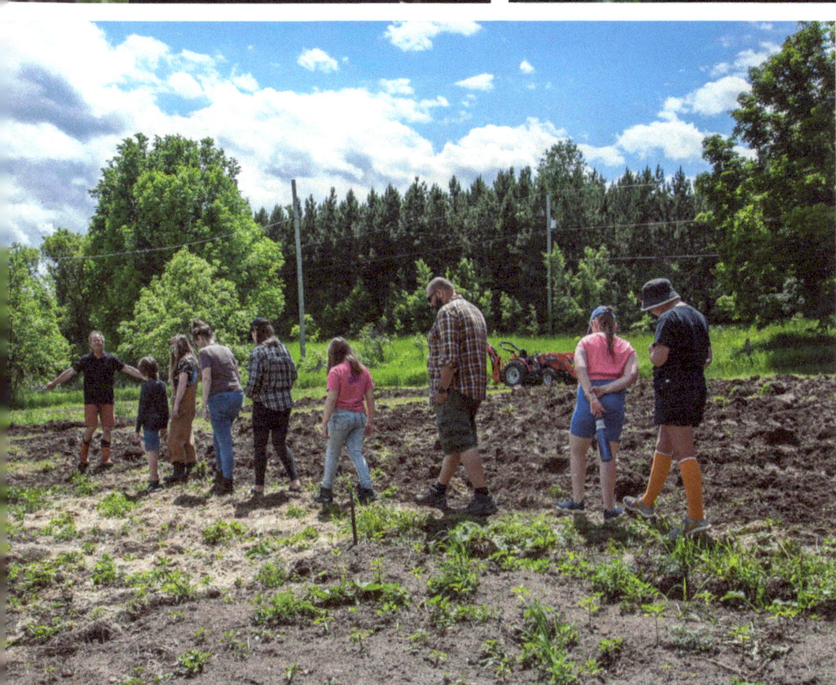

"I believe that gardening and art are not that different," said Cameron, creative director at Studio Dreamshare. "Both connect us to our instincts to play, to take joy in doing, and to engage in the deep fulfillment of slow learning and slow growing. As people it is our moral duty to understand and witness where our food comes from, especially in this paradigm where consumers are disconnected from creation. As artists we develop a richer appreciation for our crafts when we see how bees make the honey in our watercolour paints, for example, or touch the sheep whose wool we use in our fibre arts."

Studio Dreamshare experimented this summer with expanding the scope of our projects to explore different pathways to community arts. We intend to do more gardening and growing in collaboration with EcoPembroke next season to continue growing the 'seeds' we planted in 2022.

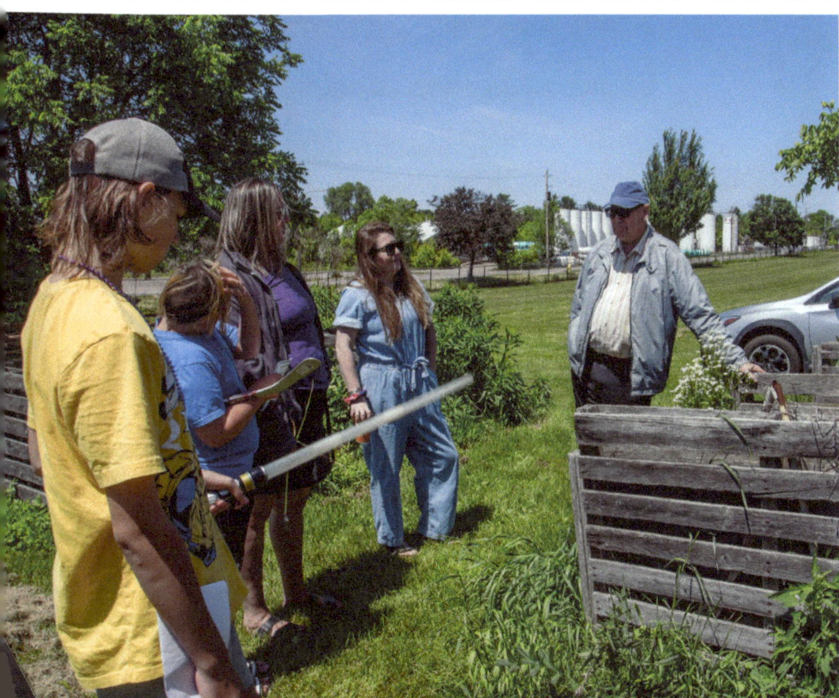

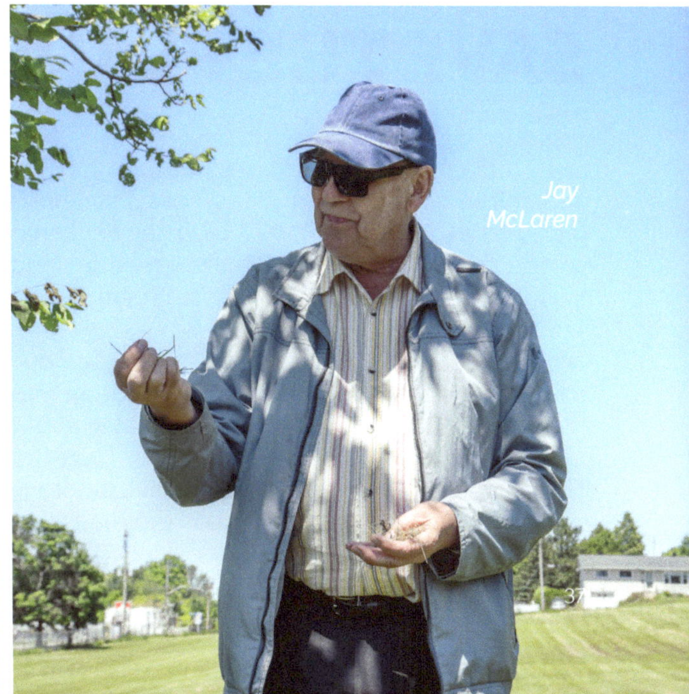

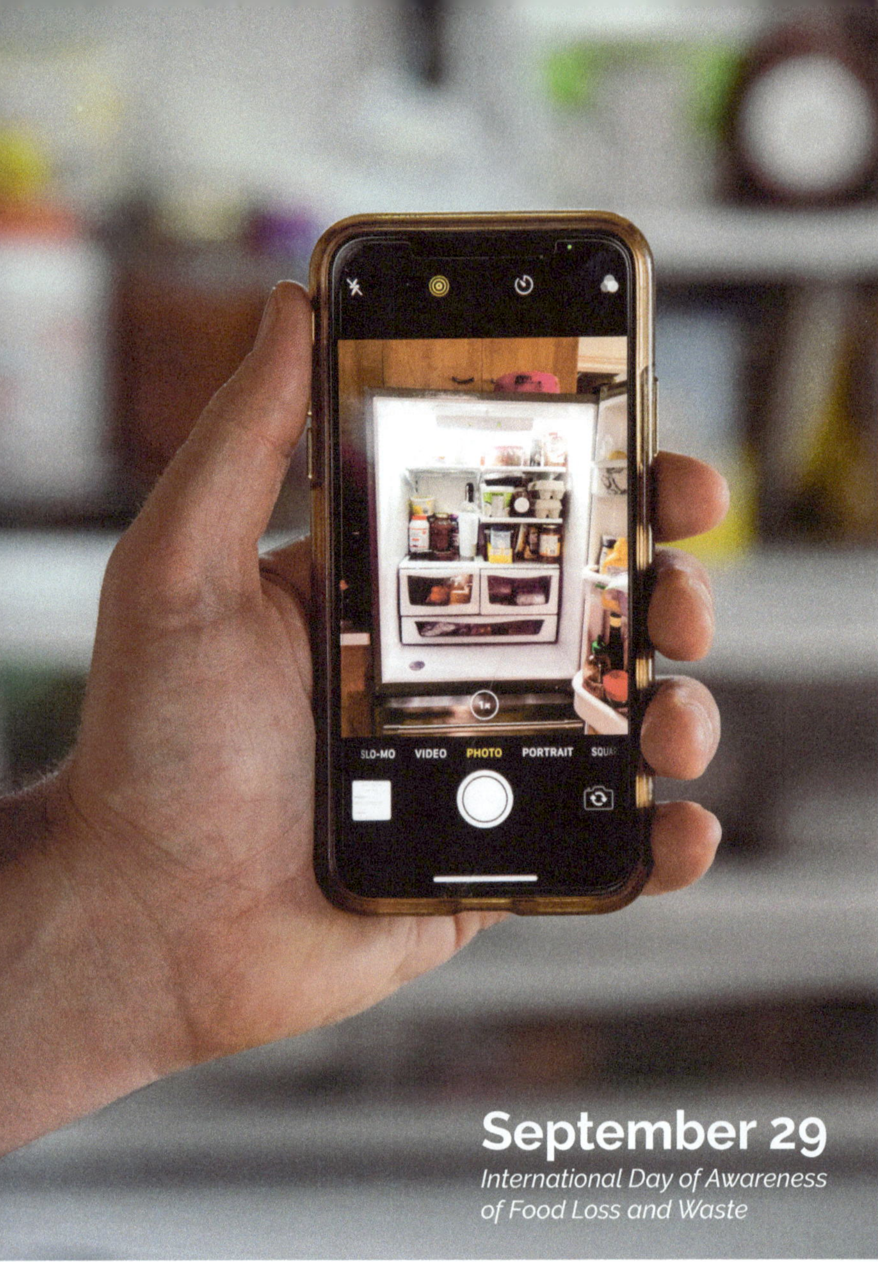

September 29
*International Day of Awareness
of Food Loss and Waste*

Take a "shelfie"

before going shopping: take a photo of the interior of your fridge and cupboard so you don't buy something you already have.

Choose one day a week to cook with leftovers or left-behind ingredients.

Save your veggie scraps (onion skins, garlic skins, pepper tops, carrot tops) to make your own **veggie stock** (save money and avoid the packaging).

Before your food rots or expires, **freeze it**, either whole or in a sauce or a dish.

Plan it out. Use it up. Keep it fresh. Consult www.lovefoodhatewaste.ca for an alphabetical reference guide to buying, storing and using food.

The environment needs a lot of people doing a little, so start small with reducing food waste.

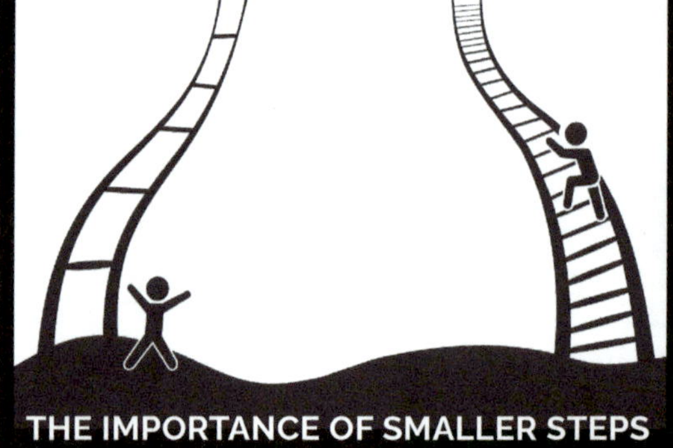

SAVE MONEY!
SAVE THE PLANET!

Did it rot before you could use it, despite your best efforts? Compost fruit, veggies, tea and coffee grounds, egg shells. For typical non-compostable foods like bones, dairy products and leftovers, buy a digester. No compost remains, but neither do the food scraps: so you have diverted that waste from landfills where it has to be processed and transported, contributing further to greenhouse gasses.

According to Canada's National Zero Waste Council, the average Canadian household throws out about 140 kilograms of food per year at a value of more than $1300 per household. What would you do with that kind of money each year???

This 2.3 million tonnes of avoidable household food waste is equivalent to 6.9 million tonnes of CO_2 or 2.1 million cars on the road.

www.lovefoodhatewaste.ca   www.nzwc.ca

You've heard about the 3 R's—Reduce, Reuse, Recycle,
but how about the 12 R's of zero waste?

Remember	why you bought it, life before it, how you could get by without it?
Respect	its value and the resources used to produce it.
Refuse	to buy/accept freebies, do you really need it?
Reduce	consumption, single-use items, car rides.
Reuse	what you already own, or share with a friend.
Return	broken goods to manufacturers, bottles and cans with deposits.
Refill	buy in bulk, refill cleaners and soaps.
Rot	compost.
Restore	what has been damaged by extracting resources?
Repurpose	use it for something else.
Repair	fix it first!
Recycle	last resort if none of the other R's apply.

Ease your eco-anxiety by
TAKING ACTION

Symphony of the Ages

Songs of the birds
Whispers from the wind
Pitter patter as the animals gather
Together a symphony
A story of harmony
For if you look closer
There is much more to this song
The underlying beat
The pulse of Mother Nature

Without sharp intervention to flatten our negative impact
We will lose elements from the orchestra
Strings will break
Off key
Out of tune
Once gone
The earth will no longer sing
The melody will fade

Silence

As individuals
As a community
Let us breathe life back into the planet
Tune ourselves
Forte
Forte
Give Earth a chance to
Crescendo
We are all instrumental
Lifestyle changes add up
A chorus worth taking
Let's sing
Let's shout
Let's make impactful changes
A symphony that transcends the ages

Naomi Fong